11758

Contents

What Do Health Visitors Do?

A Review of the Research 1960–1980

JUNE CLARK

B.A. (Hons.), M. Phil., S.R.N., H.V. Cert.

Aims of the Series

To encourage the appreciation and dissemination of nursing research by making relevant studies of high quality available to the profession at reasonable cost.

The Rcn is very happy indeed to co-operate with the Department of Health and Social Security in publishing this series of research reports. The projects were chosen by the individual research worker and the findings are those of the researcher and relate to the particular subject in the situation in which it was studied. The Rcn, in accordance with its policy of promoting research awareness among members of the profession, commends this series for study but views expressed do not necessarily reflect Rcn policy.

British Library Cataloguing in Publication Data

Clark, June
  What do health visitors do?
  1. Home nursing
  2. Medical care — Great Britain
  I. Title
  362.1'4'0941   HV248

ISBN 0-902606-63-8

Published by
The Royal College of Nursing of the United Kingdom,
Henrietta Place, Cavendish Square, London, W1M 0AB

PRINTED BY THE WHITEFRIARS PRESS LTD.,
LONDON AND TONBRIDGE

8336

List of Tables

Acknowledgements

Thanks are due to the Department of Health and Social Security who financed this project;

to Grace Owen, Kate Robinson, and Sheila Jack—my colleagues at the Polytechnic of the South Bank—who made invaluable comments on the manuscript;

to Pat O'Brien, who undertook the administrative work of tracing and contacting the original researchers;

to Valerie Joyce who typed the original version, and Stephanie Sherfield who typed the final manuscript;

and, most of all, to my husband Roger, without whose support I could achieve nothing; and my children, Andrew and Gillian, who somehow survive the deprivations associated with having a working mum.

CHAPTER 1

Introduction:
Plan and Method of the
Review

This review is an attempt to collate and evaluate the information available to date about the work of the health visitor. It is hoped that a summary of the existing state of knowledge will be useful as a "source book" both for those who make the policy decisions which affect the health visiting service, and also for those who wish to undertake further research in this field. For the policy makers it is important that decisions take into account the best information available about the reality of health visiting practice as well as the role prescriptions and professional aspirations which, particularly while health visiting resources remain inadequate for the demands placed upon them, may be far removed from the reality of health visiting practice. For research workers who are planning or undertaking further studies of the work of the health visitor, knowledge of previous work is essential to the choice of the research strategy, the tools for data collection, and the methods of analysis and presentation of data in ways which will make the findings comparable with those of other studies and relevant and meaningful to other people. It is hoped that this review will also draw attention to the gaps in existing knowledge and suggest useful hypotheses for further research.

Thirty-seven studies are included in this review. (Table 1). Many of them would not claim for themselves the title of "research"; they have been included because in a field where so little information is available even the smallest of studies may make an important contribution. The search strategy aimed to include any material which fell within the broad definition of research as "the collection of data in a rigorously controlled situation for the purpose of prediction or explanation" (Treece and Treece, 1973). The inadequacies and imperfections in these studies are not always the result of "small scale" but are often the result of lack of rigour in the "rigorously controlled situation"; these problems are discussed in Chapter 2.

Details of published studies were obtained by a thorough manual search of the British literature since 1960 and a computer search (MEDLINE via BLAISE) of world literature as indexed by Index Medicus. Details of unpublished work were obtained by means of

7

Table 1

Summary of 37 Studies of the Work of the Health Visitor

Study	Name of Researcher	Date of Study	Location of Study	Sample	
				No. of H.Vs	Duration
1	Akester and MacPhail	1961	Leeds	51	1 week
2	Allen and King	a) 1965	Hertfordshire	23	1 month
		b) 1966		30	1 month
3	Allen, King and Abbott	1969	Hertfordshire	143	1 month
4	Ambler et al	1967	3 unidentified towns	51	1 week
5	Atkinson	1970	West Riding Yorkshire	263	6 weeks
6	Carter	1971	National Sample	20	1 week
7	City of Leicester	1968–1969	Leicester	29	4 weeks
8	Clark	1969	Berkshire	72	1 week
9	Clow	1966	West Riding Yorkshire	48	1 week
10	Dawtrey	1976	London	2	1 year
11	Ellwood and Jeffereys	1971–1972	London	11	1 year
12	Fry et al	1963–1964	Surrey	1	1 year
13	Gallaher et al	1966	Bolton	40	4 weeks
14	Gettings (a)	1966–1967	Berkshire	1	1 year
15	Gettings (b)	1969	Berkshire	Not Given	1 month
16	Gilmore	1967–1968	Brighton	2	2 weeks (visit records = 1 year)
17	Gilmore et al	1972–1973	Scotland	9	4 weeks (visit records = 3 months)
18	Graham	1965	Worthing	8	4 months
19	Henderson	1975	Hampshire	183	2 weeks
20	Jeffereys	1961	Buckinghamshire	46	1 week

8

Table 1 (continued)

Summary of 37 Studies of the Work of the Health Visitor (continued)

Study	Name of Researcher	Date of Study	Location of Study	Sample	
				No. of H.Vs	Duration
21	Loveland	1968	Wiltshire & London	91	4 weeks
22	Marris	1969	London	215	2 weeks
23	Ministry of Health (Jameson Report)	1954	National Sample	77	1 week
24	Morris	1975	Preston	62	1 month
25	Naidoo	1976	London	11	3 weeks
26	Nimmo	1978	Aberdeen	1	7 sessions
27	Nimmo	1979	Aberdeen	1	7 sessions
28	Potton	1977–1978	Kent	134	1 week
29	Poulton	1976	London	38	1 week
30	Thorpe	1978	London	6	Not Given
31	Thurmott	1973	Hertfordshire	61	1 week
32	Walworth-Bell	1978	London	70	4 weeks
33	Watson	1976	Aberdeen	21	4 days
34	White	1971	Cardiff	Not Given	2 days
35	Wilkes & Nimmo	1973–1974	Grampian Health Board	8	2 weeks
36	Wiseman	1978	Blackpool	25	40 days
37	Young	1969–1970	Scotland	20	1 week

9

responses to a letter sent by the Professional Adviser (Research) of the C.E.T.H.V. to all Area Nursing Officers in the U.K. asking for details of recent or ongoing research, responses to a similar letter by the reviewer published in the April 1978 issue of the journal "Health Visitor", and by personal contacts.

It was decided to limit the review to studies undertaken in the United Kingdom, partly because of the difficulty, common to many fields, of drawing valid inferences from data relating to services and situations which are very different from those which exist in the United Kingdom, but mainly because health visiting is in fact peculiar to the United Kingdom and is not directly comparable with the "public health nursing" of other countries.

It was originally decided to include only studies published or undertaken since 1970, on the grounds that earlier work would have been included by Hawthorn in her review "The Nurse Working With The General Practitioner" (D.H.S.S. 1971). However, some earlier seminal work, e.g. the work undertaken for the Working Party on the Field of Work, Training and Recruitment of Health Visitors which published its report, known as the Jameson Report, in 1956, had not been included by Hawthorn, and it was considered important that such data should be included as a baseline with which later findings could be compared. For the sake of completeness the five relevant studies which were reviewed by Hawthorn are also included in this review.

Only material based on original empirical work is included in this review. Articles which discuss other people's research findings or "the role of the health visitor" but which do not present any research data have not been included. A further limit is that only data which describes directly the work of the health visitor has been included; studies which were concerned with other aspects of health visiting (e.g. recruitment and training), or based on the opinions of health visitors about their work (e.g. opinions about attachment) have not been included. In these two respects this review differs from both those of Hawthorn (1971) and Hicks (1976). Within these limits the review attempts to be comprehensive, but of course it is almost inevitable that there are other studies of which the reviewer is unaware.

The review is divided into two main parts. In the main body of the review the findings of all (or as many as possible) of the studies on a single area of subject matter are collated and where possible compared. Thus Chapter 3 draws together all the findings on the allocation of time to various kinds of health visiting activity, Chapter 4 all the information about the health visitor's clientele, and so on to Chapter 13 which attempts to draw together the data relating to the effect of attachment to general practice. Then each study is separately summarised, using the same framework for each, and the summaries are collected together and arranged alphabetically by the name of the author to form the main appendix (Appendix B). An introductory chapter (Chapter 2) discusses the methodological problems and the limitations which they place on the interpretation of the data; and a final chapter (Chapter 14) discusses the overall situation and offers some suggestions for future research. Wherever possible the summaries were prepared by the authors of the individual studies. Where it was not possible to trace the original researcher, the summary was prepared by the reviewer; these summaries are marked with an asterisk. The main text, however, was not discussed with original researchers, and responsibility for any errors or mis-interpretations, therefore, rests with the reviewer.

CHAPTER 2

Problems and Limitations of the Research

Research has been categorised by various authors in various ways, but an approach which combines that of French (1968) and Hyman (1955) distinguishes the following four types of research:

(i) exploratory research: in which the investigator studies a situation to find out which variables are important to making the situation what it is;

(ii) descriptive research: in which the investigator studies the variables, the frequency with which they occur in a given situation and perhaps the correlations between them;

(iii) explanatory research: ⎫ in which the investigator studies the
(iv) experimental research: ⎭ effect of the variables on one another.

The aims of explanatory and experimental research are somewhat similar in that both test hypothesised *causal* relationships between variables; but explanatory research, unlike the experiment, does not involve manipulation of the variables, nor does it have the characteristic ability of the experimental design to control or to randomise all extraneous variables.

These four types of research are distinct; each requires its own strategy, design and methods; and each has its own uses and limitations. Moreover, the four types form a logical hierarchy; since evaluative research, whether explanatory or experimental, requires careful specification of the variables to be studied, it cannot logically precede descriptive research, and descriptive research cannot logically precede exploratory research. As Krausz and Miller (1974) suggest:

"The type of objective one adopts depends on the existing state of knowledge in the field. If there is little relevant knowledge, an exploratory study will be in order. If the researcher already has a good idea of the important variables in a problem area, he is likely to conduct an explanatory study. In either case the defining of objectives is important because it helps to clarify and direct an investigation; and because by looking at the objectives it is possible to assess whether the problem is really manageable with available skills and resources". (Krausz and Miller, 1974, Page 10).

In research relating to the work of the health visitor, however, these different types of research, and in particular, their distinctive uses and limitations, have become confused. None of the 37 studies included in this review could be properly categorised as evaluative research, although several include the word "evaluation" in their stated aims, and one (No. 26) claims it in the title. Only one (No. 32) could be included in Hyman's "explanatory" category, in which the objective takes the form of a hypothesis (or set of hypotheses) to be tested; and even this study does not exhibit the methodological rigour which is required for hypothesis testing. It is therefore important to recognise that while the data presented may be of interest in their own right and useful in certain limited situations, the type of research approach and the level of rigour of the methodology do not permit the generalisations and conclusions which have sometimes been drawn.

As Oppenheim (1966) remarks:

> "Too often surveys are carried out on the basis of insufficient design and planning or on the basis of no design at all. 'Fact-gathering' can be an exciting and tempting activity to which a questionnaire opens a quick and seemingly easy avenue; the weaknesses in the design are frequently not realised until the results have to be interpreted—if then! Survey literature abounds with portentious conclusions based on faulty inferences from insufficient evidence wrongly assembled and misguidedly collected". (Oppenheim, 1966, Page 3).

This assessment certainly applies to the research into the work of the health visitor. For example, the review of the studies concerned with the attachment of health visitors to general practice (Chapter 13) suggests that the research evidence is inadequate to be used either to support or to oppose the policy of attachment.

The research to date has relied almost exclusively on survey methods. One study (No. 33) has used observation, and one (No. 10) used a documentary approach. Survey methods are widely used in social research. Their main strength is their ability to collect a large amount of data from a large number of people with the minimum amount of personal supervision by the research worker; they are therefore attractive because of their economy of research time and research money.

Like all methods, survey methods have their own inherent limitations. In particular, information about the health visitor's work obtained by means of questionnaires or self-recorded work records is always secondary and therefore subject to error as a result of factors such as memory recall, misunderstanding the question, and conscious or unconscious distortion of replies. As Sir Claus Moser, one of the greatest exponents of survey methodology remarks:

> "I have tried also to stress the limitations of the survey approach and to caution potential users against an uncritical faith in its power ... With the social survey, as with any scientific method, part of the skill lies in knowing when to use it at all". (Moser and Kalton, 1958, Preface).

An even greater problem for the present review, however, is that surveys of the work of the health visitor which have been undertaken to date are singularly deficient in the methodological rigour on which the strength of survey research depends. Moreover, attempts to assess the methodological rigour as a pre-requisite to assessing the findings are impeded by poor reporting. Few of the research reports in this review, published or unpublished, meet Stacey's criteria of "Minimum items to include in a social research report" (Stacey, 1969, Appendix 1). For example, details of the sample and the response rates are frequently omitted; instruments are rarely reproduced and are not always described. The main limitations upon the data included in this review concern:

1. the samples from which the data was collected
2. the instruments used to collect the data
3. the organisation of the data collection and the manner in which work was undertaken
4. the analysis and presentation of the data.

1. The Samples from which the Data were Collected:

The quantity of data generated by a study of the work of the health visitor is determined by the number of respondents, the length of time during which the work was recorded, and the depth of detail of the material. The first two of these factors together constitute what is loosely, and rather inaccurately, referred to in the summaries of the studies as presented in Appendix B as "the sample". This rather loose usage of the term confuses the two distinct statistical terms "population" and "sample". The term "population" or "universe" denotes "the aggregate of units to which the survey results are to apply" or the "total number of units of enquiry"; the term "sample" denotes a part of the "universe", determined by some form of carefully controlled selection. A detailed account of precise terminology and of the theory and practice of sampling is contained in Moser and Kalton (1971). The surveys of the work of the health visitor included in this review covered either all the health visitors in a particular area—which might be termed a "population" although it is only a part of the total population of health visitors—or a number of health visitors in one or more areas chosen by the researcher. The numbers of health visitors covered ranged from one to 263; the length of the survey period ranged from two days to one year.

It is often suggested that the size of the "sample" limits the value of small-scale research findings. This is not necessarily true; it depends entirely on the purpose of the research and the use to which the findings are to be put. In any case the size of the sample is far less important than the manner in which it is chosen. As Krausz and Miller (1974) point out:

"The basic premise in sampling a universe is that the selection of a relatively small number of units on a scientifically arranged random basis will provide a sufficiently high degree of probability that it is a true reflection of the universe, that inferences may be made from the findings of the sample to the universe which is being scrutinised ... that enables the researcher to generalise within known limits of error from the sample to the population". (Krausz and Miller, 1974, Page 32).

In short, where there is no intention to generalise from the survey's findings sampling is irrelevant; conversely if generalisations are to be made, the sampling must be rigorous.

Not all the studies included in this review give precise details either of the sample or the methods used to determine it. Very few record response rates, a factor which is as important as the method of sampling. It is, however, noteworthy that where response rates are reported (e.g. No. 8 and No. 19) they are high in comparison with most survey research. No study to date has used a sample from which we can legitimately generalise about health visiting over the country as a whole. Moreover, because of the tremendous variety of health visiting practice and the great number of variables which would have to be taken into account, such a sample would probably be very large and very difficult to achieve. A survey of the work of community nurses (including health visitors) which is being undertaken during 1980 by the Office of Population Censuses and Surveys may go some way towards repairing this deficit.

2. Organisation and Method of Data Collection

The accuracy and completeness of the data collected by survey methods depends greatly on the control which is exercised over the manner of its collection. Although few of the research reports include much information about the organisation of the data collection, certain deficiencies are clearly apparent in some studies and must be suspected in others.

Two factors are particularly relevant to studies of the work of the health visitor.

(a) the demand of time and effort which the research makes upon the respondent.

Where the demand is excessive (i.e. considered by the respondent to be excessive) there will be under-recording, selectivity and inaccuracy in the data obtained. A difficult or complicated recording instrument will increase the demand. The demand involved in self-recording and particularly in self-timing any continuous activity is very great, and this method of recording health visiting activity in particular poses very considerable problems, both because of the complex nature of the activity itself, and because of the pressure of work under which health visitors currently operate.

(b) the independence of the research.

Where a study is carried out by an employing authority, particularly by nursing management, it is inevitable that the field level respondents will seek, albeit unconciously, to present themselves and their work in a way which they believe will appear "favourable" to their superiors. The protection normally afforded to respondents by anonymity and confidentiality is also put at risk. The greatest "threat" of all to a respondent is the belief, whether erroneous or not, that the data will be "used against him", e.g. in some form of personal appraisal or "performance targets". It is for this reason that work study is almost universally carried out by independent observers (which minimises "favourable" distortion) and is dependent on prior negotiation with organisations such as trade unions which are specifically concerned to protect the staff's interests. The distortion which such lack of independence causes must be suspected in all the studies carried out by employing authorities, particularly those involving performance targets. Surprisingly, a number of independent research workers also jeopardised their data by using nursing management—frequently their respondents' immediate superiors—to distribute and collect their questionnaires and work records.

3. The Instruments to Collect the Data

The development of survey instruments is a difficult task which demands considerable knowledge and skill—a fact which is insufficiently appreciated by many inexperienced researchers. Oppenheim (1966) remarks:

"The world is full of well-meaning people who believe that anyone who can write plain English and has a modicum of common sense can produce a good questionnaire".

Even a good questionnaire has its limitations, and there are many examples in the 37 studies reviewed of abuse of the questionnaire method. For example, a questionnaire which asks respondents to state how much time they spent on various categories of activity during the previous week is a poor method of finding the required information.

The development of an instrument to measure health visiting activity is a particularly difficult task. The most accurate and objective method of recording work activity is by means of direct observation, and this is almost universally used in the study of other kinds of work. Observation is, however, much more expensive than survey methods and cannot be applied to large samples; moreover, observation of health visiting activity presents special problems because health visiting consists largely of person-to-person interaction in private settings. Only one study to date, that of Watson (No. 33), has used observational methods.

The great majority of the studies have used some form of self-recorded "work-schedule". The special problems of this method are firstly the implications of self-recording, and secondly the implications of recording time.

Any self-recorded instrument produces data which are secondary—not what the health visitor did, but what she remembers of what she thought she did, or even what she thinks the researcher would expect her to have done. Moser and Kalton (1971) point out:

"Any informant may give a false reply because he misunderstands the question or because consciously or unconsciously, he distorts his answer; the latter can occur for a variety of reasons, such as the desire of prestige or the desire by the informant to give the answer he thinks is expected of him". (Moser and Kalton, 1971, Page 246).

In recording work, factors of prestige and other people's expectations are likely to be important, particularly if the study is being undertaken by one's employer or work superior. Self-recording time is particularly difficult because the recording itself constitutes an interruption in the activity, and if activities follow one another in rapid succession or are at all complex, demanding considerable concentration, the conflict between the demands of doing the work and the demands of recording it may become intolerable, if only at an unconscious level. One mechanism for resolving the conflict is to defer the recording activity until later; recording done in retrospect is notoriously inaccurate. Another mechanism, which may be unconscious, is partial or under-recording; this is particularly dangerous not only because it makes the picture incomplete but also because it may be unconscious and, therefore, unrecognised, and because the selection which is involved will vary from respondent to respondent. When time is recorded and categorised in detail as opposed to broad outline there are also problems for the analysis of the data.

The effect of these problems is most evident in the work of Marris (Study No. 22). In this study the demands made upon the respondents were considerable; they were expected to record all their activities for a period of two weeks, using a very elaborate schedule, in which they were expected to record the time allocated to each activity (the average length of an activity was 13·1 minutes) and, within each activity, to each person served and each topic discussed. The assumptions which were necessary for the analysis of the data obtained are further discussed in Chapter 12 but his finding that "the commonest number of topics covered with a person was one" is so far removed from everyday experience that it must be taken as an indication of a considerable degree of under-recording, while the extent of the data lost and the resulting bias in the data obtained is impossible to assess.

Apart from these special problems of self-recorded work schedules, all questionnaires and schedules involve the allocation of data to various categories, either by the respondent (using a pre-coded schedule) or subsequently by the researcher. Almost all the instruments used in the 37 studies reviewed were precoded.

For any item of subject matter (variable) there must be enough categories to cover the full range of responses and to provide a distillation of the responses without loss of meaning, but not so many that it is difficult to choose between them or difficult to grasp the range of responses as a whole. There must be a category for every single response, and a response must fit into one category and (generally) one category only; that is, the list must be exhaustive, and the categories must (generally) be mutually exclusive. They must "make sense", taking into account the nature of the data and the purpose for which it is to be used; that is, they must be valid. And the categories must be such that a particular response is allocated to the same category regardless of who is doing the allocation; that is, they must be reliable.

At present we have no category system for the classification of any aspect of health visiting which fulfills all these essential criteria. Moreover, among the 37 studies reviewed, no two studies use the same category system so that direct comparison of findings between studies is rarely possible, and in many of the studies the categories used are neither exhaustive nor mutually exclusive.

This problem is most evident in the attempts to categorise the health visitor's visits by "type". In many studies a single category system incorporates clientele (categorised by age or by a diagnostic label), the source of the visit, and the purpose of the visit. The categories are, therefore, not mutually exclusive, and, since residual categories such as "other" or "not known" are not always offered, they are frequently not exhaustive. For example, one study incorporates into a single category system headed "Location/type of visit" the categories "crisis intervention", "families with problems", "problem familes", "follow-up from hospital", "handicapped child", "immigrant visits", "new parent (support)". It would be an extreme case, but it is quite possible that a single visit could be placed in all seven categories. Sometimes the categories are vague or open to crude subjective definition; for example, one study uses the category "family domestic problem" which is defined as "situations where your visit involves more than just the child or for older patients other members of the family".

Error is always possible when the respondent is asked to mark one category among a given list. The risk is greatly increased where the respondent is asked to select a numerical code from a code list before marking it in the schedule, particularly if the code lists are long. Marris' respondents were required to select and record the appropriate numbers for each activity (24 categories), person (37 categories), topic (38 categories) and technique (15 categories). This method also precludes the identification of errors at the stage of editing the schedules.

None of the instruments used was adequately tested for reliability or validity, and few studies included a pilot study which would have excluded some of the most obvious errors.

4. Analysis and Presentation of Data

Once collected, data must be sorted, counted, summarised and presented in such a way as to be meaningful to the reader. Computer systems and statistical techniques are available to assist both in the description of data and in the drawing of inferences from it. It is important to appreciate, however, that statistical analysis, however sophisticated, cannot improve the raw data. The use of refined methods of analysis on crude data may

18

give results a misleading appearance of precision and the research itself a spurious respectability. On the other hand the presentation of data as raw scores, particularly when the numbers involved are large, makes interpretation of the findings difficult. Both of these errors are apparent in the studies included in this review.

Several studies present their data as raw scores only, without calculating percentages. This makes comparisons difficult, both within studies (comparisons between sub-groups) and between studies. Conversely some studies present percentages without raw scores, even without giving the raw total on which the percentage is calculated; this can be very misleading, particularly when the raw total is less than 100 or where the calculation to several decimal places gives the appearance of precision.

The simplest and most widely used statistic for summarising data is the arithmetic mean (commonly called the average). A few studies report the mode. The measures of central tendency are, however, difficult to interpret without a measure of dispersion, such as the standard deviation. A few studies report ranges and one (No. 18) reports only the range.

Where comparative data is presented in order to demonstrate differences, some means of assessing the significance of the difference is required. There is an important distinction to be drawn, however, between substantive significance and statistical significance. Tests of statistical significance depend greatly on sample size; the larger the sample the greater the chance that a difference of a given size will be found to be statistically significant. In findings based on small samples, such as most of the studies included in this review, differences which are not large enough to be statistically significant may nevertheless be important (i.e. have substantive significance). Conversely the application of a statistical test to poor quality data may produce a statistical difference which is nevertheless spurious. Both types of error are evident in the studies relating to the effect of attachment (Chapter 13). In the end the reader must base his judgements on his assessment of the overall quality of the research and his interpretation of the meaning of its findings.

Whether it is subjected to statistical analysis or not, data must be presented in a way which is meaningful to the reader. Graphic presentation is helpful, provided it is honest (i.e. not distorted by the use of inappropriate techniques or scales), but it is inadequate when used alone. In some of the studies carried out by researchers who were not health visitors, the method of presentation chosen, while perfectly accurate, is not very meaningful for the average health visitor reader; for example, an injudicious choice of percentage base can make good raw scores meaningless. In several of the studies the tabular presentation is poor, the headings are imprecise, and the material included is inadequate for proper interpretation.

This methodological critique of the studies covered by this review is included not in order to undermine the value of the research, but in order

19

that its limitations may be clearly recognised and taken into account in the interpretation of the data recorded. I hope also that, by drawing attention to the mistakes of previous research, it will help future researchers to avoid some of the many pitfalls.

CHAPTER 3

How the Health Visitor Spends Her Time

Twenty-five of the thirty-seven studies investigated the proportion of time spent by respondents on various activities; for some this was the main purpose of the study. Their findings are summarised in Table 2. In very general terms it is possible to conclude that health visitors spend between a quarter and a third of their time on home visits, about a sixth on clinic sessions (mainly child health sessions), a further sixth on travelling, and about a quarter on clerical work.

Table 2 permits some comparison of the allocation of time as recorded by several studies, but should be interpreted with considerable caution. In addition to the overall limitations imposed by the use of self-recording and especially self-timing, comparison between the studies also requires caution. The study areas vary widely in population structure, geography and working arrangements; the sample sizes also vary widely and some samples were very small.

Comparison is further inhibited by the use of different category systems; where possible some explanation has been included in the Notes. The effect of this problem is clearly shown in the final column where the proportion of time recorded under the residual category "Other" is often very high, in some cases higher than any other category. This inevitably distorts the proportions recorded in the other categories: whenever a percentage of the data is allocated to an additional category, the percentages in the other categories are inevitably reduced because percentages are proportions of a finite total (i.e. 100 per cent). So, for example, if the category system of a study requires data to be included in one of the four categories: home visits, clinic sessions, travelling, and clerical/administration, it is likely that time spent on meetings or consultation with colleagues will be allocated to "clerical/administration" as the most general category. If the same raw data is allocated to the five categories: home visits, clinic sessions, travelling, clerical/administrative and meetings/consultations, time spent on meetings and consultations will be allocated to the fifth category and the percentage of time recorded as "clerical/administrative" will be correspondingly reduced, even though the raw data is identical. The use of a residual category labelled "Other" permits much greater accuracy in respect of the main categories, even where a high percentage allocated to

Table 2

How the Health Visitor Spends her Time: Percentages of Total Working Time Allocated to Four Broad Categories of Activity (25 studies)

Study No.	Date of Study	Name of researcher	Visits	Clinics	Admin/ Clerical	Travel	Other
22	1955	Min. of Health (Jameson Rep.)	29·7	29·2	11·4	15·6	14·1
1	1961	Akester & MacPhail	26·8	27·4	27·5[1]	15·5	2·8
19	1961	Jefferys	55·0[2]	16·0	27·0	—[2]	2·0
17	1965	Graham[3]	48·3	15·3	24·8	13·4	15·1
2	1965-66	Allen & King[4]	29·0	13·0	20·0	12·0	26·0
12	1966	Gallaher et al	17·0	19·0	20·0	15·0	29·0
8	1966	Clow	37·1	15·8	19·9[1]	17·2	9·9
4	1967	Ambler et al	33·5	19·7	28·9	5·2[5]	12·7
15	1967-68	Gilmore	35·2	2·1	48·0[6]	10·0	4·7
20	1968	Loveland	58·1	12·3	20·2	—[7]	9·4
7	1968-69	City of Leicester	20·8	14·9	41·9[1]	13·1	3·2
21	1969	Marris	17·5	13·9	23·8	10·5	34·3
3	1969	Allen, King & Abbott	29·3	9·6	22·4	11·7	27·0
36	1969-70	Young[8]	42·0	22·0	28·0	19·0	—[8]
5	1970	Atkinson	25·2	17·4	25·1	13·6	18·7
31	1971	White	21·7	9·0	30·4[1]	12·7	26·2
32	1971-72	Wilkes & Nimmo	25·0	15·0	30·0	13·6	16·4
6	1971-72	Carter	32·2	15·3[9]	24·0	16·0	12·5
16	1972-73	Gilmore et al	25·0	16·6	20·6	9·0	28·8
28	1973	Thurmott	34·6	13·1	26·6	11·9	13·8
30	1975	Watson	27·0	8·0	33·0	19·0	13·0
18	1975	Henderson	23·0	12·0	21·0	14·0	30·0
23	1975	Morris	39·7	11·3	26·5	—	22·5
26	1976	Poulton[8]	25·6	18·2	51·7	12·6	—
25	1977	Potton	24·4	14·4	24·2	16·1	20·9
		Mean	31·3	15·2	27·1	13·5	17·0

Notes to Table 2
1. Admin/clerical includes time telephoning.
2. Jefferys included travelling time with visiting time.
3. Graham reported ranges; these figures calculated as mid-point of range.
4. "Triple-duty workers" excluded.
5. Ambler excluded travelling times of less than 10 minutes.
6. Admin/clerical time includes meetings and discussions with colleagues.
7. Loveland did not ask for travelling time to be recorded separately.
8. Figures total more than 100 per cent because figures are based on composite of "activity" and "place" categories.
9. "Clinics" = working with patients in surgery.

Table 3

The Health Visitor's "Average Working Day" (5 studies)

Activity	Study No. 1 Akester and McPhail		Study No. 2 Allen and King[2]		Study No. 22 Marris		Study No. 19 Henderson		Study No. 29 Poulton	
	hrs	mins	hrs	mins	hrs	mins	hrs	mins	hrs	mins
Home visits	2	56	2	21	1	30	1	57	2	03
Clinic sessions	see note 1			56	1	11	1	06	1	31
Group Health Education	Not recorded			15	Not recorded			15	Not recorded	
Other Client Contact		5		37		36		20	Not recorded	
Travelling	1	37		52		54	1	11	1	0
Meetings & Consultation	Not recorded			27		53		51	Not recorded	
Clerical/Admin	2	30[3]	1	40	2	03	1	47	3	26[7]
Other		2		11		35		20		0
Total	7	10[4]	7	21	7	42[5]	7	47[6]	8	0

Notes to Table 3

1. Data for 93 days with no clinic sessions; average day for days with clinic sessions (138 days) not given.
2. Mean of attached and non-attached health visitors.
3. Includes 12 minutes telephoning.
4. Total obtained by addition (not given in original table); total reported in text is 7 hours 14 minutes.
5. Excluding 55 minutes recorded meal-breaks.
6. Excluding 41 minutes recorded meal-breaks.
7. At base 1 hour 46 minutes; at other places 1 hour 40 minutes.

23

the "Other" category indicates that the total category system is insufficiently detailed. Where a detailed and precise category system has been used for the original data it is relatively easy to add together categories to form broader categories according to criteria which can be specified. Unfortunately, however, even where the categories used by the respondents are relatively precise, in the final report the categories may be grouped together by the report-writer without specifying the criteria used for grouping, or into groups which are different from those used in other studies. In these cases it may be extremely difficult to interpret the findings of any study and impossible to compare the findings of one with those of another.

The studies are arranged in chronological order to permit comparison over a period of about twenty years. The evidence of Table 2 does not support the popular view of a trend away from home visiting or towards increased travelling time or increased clerical work, at least within the last decade. Indeed no clear trends or changes over time are immediately apparent except possibly (see Chapter 11) an increase in the time devoted to meetings and consultations with colleagues.

Table 3 presents the same raw data in terms of health visitor's "average working day". It must be appreciated that these figures are ob-

Table 4

How the Health Visitor Spends her Time: Percentage of Total Working Time Spent in Direct Contact with Clients (11 studies)

				% of total working time	
Study No.	Name of Researcher	Date of Study	No. of H.Vs	Client Contact	Ancillary Activities
1	Akester and MacPhail	1961	51	57	43
20	Jefferys	1961	46	67 (estimate)	33 (estimate)
4	Ambler *et al*	1966	54	61	37
13	Gallaher *et al*	1966	40	65	35
7	City of Leicester	1968-69	29	41·5	58·5
22	Marris	1969	215	38	62
35	Wilkes and Nimmo	1969-70	20	53	47
5	Atkinson	1970	264	50·4	49·6
37	Young[1]	1971	20	53[1]	47[1]
19	Henderson	1975	183	43	57
29	Poulton	1976	83	31	69

Notes to Table 4

1. These figures relate to the first survey; after the introduction of performance targets which follow the survey the proportions were:

        Client Contact   74%

        Ancillary Activities   26%

tained by statistical manipulation of the overall totals, so that the term "average" means "statistical mean" and not "typical". For instance, the time allocated to clinic sessions and group health education is inevitably distorted by the relative infrequency of the sessions. Wilkes and Nimmo (Study No. 35) noted that the workload of health visitors varied considerably from day to day, and that the health visitors, unlike the district nurses, appeared to regulate their work on a weekly rather than daily basis.

Table 4 shows the proportion of time spent in direct contact with clients compared with that spent on ancillary activities. Although the methodological problems already mentioned make interpretation difficult, it does appear that the proportion of time spent in direct client contact has fallen during the past two decades. This conflicts with the evidence of Table 2 which is based on a different category system. The discrepancy may be due simply to the differences in category systems, or to the inclusion of "indirect" contact in categories such as clinic sessions (e.g. clinic preparation, clearing or administration), or to the effect of using vague categories such as "liason" and the possible increase over time in "meetings and consultation".

Discussion:

These findings must be regarded with considerable caution. With the sole exception of Watson's study (No. 33) whose data were recorded by an independent observer using a stop-watch, all the findings are based on the respondents' own self-recorded estimates. Some studies used a work study type proforma in which the start times or start and finish times of each activity were recorded by the respondent simultaneously with each change of activity, others base their findings on daily or weekly summaries, and a few relied on the health visitor's estimates obtained by means of retrospective interview or questionnaire. In most cases the inadequacy of the methodological detail included in the research report makes assessment of the data extremely difficult.

It is notoriously difficult to time one's own activity accurately, particularly when, as in health visiting, the activity itself is complex and requires considerable concentration, and it is perhaps significant that orthodox work study as applied in industry always uses trained observers. This problem was discussed in Chapter 2. To obtain any degree of accuracy records of start or finish times of activities which may last only a few minutes must be recorded simultaneoulsy with the change of activity. The City of Leicester (Study No. 7) minimised this problem by using tape recorders instead of a written schedule. Marris (1971) reports:

"The best way to fill in diary sheet was throughout the day, so that each activity was recorded as soon after it was finished as possible. Many health visitors followed this suggested method leaving only a few activities to be

25

recorded at the end of the day, perhaps when writing up and filing case notes and so on. However, there were a few health visitors who left all the recording on the diary sheets to the end of the day or to the end of two days' work, and a very few who completed the whole lot over the weekend ... There were one sixth of all the health visitors whose records show that they filled in some or all of their diary sheets in this way". (Marris, 1971, Page 9).

Unless such records are properly completed their reliability is doubtful, and their apparent precision spurious.

It is important to note, also, that the moral overtones, feelings of guilt (however unnecessary), desire for prestige, desire to give the expected answer, desire to please, etc., are probably greater in questions relating to the use of an employer's time than in most other fields, particularly when (as in several of the studies) the data are to be directly returned to (and, therefore, possibly scrutinised by) the employer in the shape of the respondent's immediate superior or nurse manager.

Quite apart from the difficulties of assessing the validity of these findings, careful interpretation is also required. The whole subject of the deployment of health visiting time is coloured by value judgements about how health visiting time *ought* to be spent. The terms "high" or "low" or, even more dangerously, "too high" or "too low", are frequently applied to report findings. It is sometimes implied (e.g. Hicks 1976, page 288) that time spent in direct client contact is "good" and should, therefore, be "high", time spent on certain "indirect" activities such as "liason" or "consultation with colleagues" is grudgingly agreed to be essential but definitely less "worthy", while time spent on clerical duties is "bad" and should, therefore, be as low as possible. While such professional judgements are important, they should be recognised as value judgements based on assumptions which may need to be questioned, tested, and perhaps even abandoned.

Meanwhile, it may prove useful to compare the allocation of health visitors' time with that of social workers (Table 5). While both groups appear to spend similar proportions of their time on travelling and on clerical duties, social workers appear to be spending substantially more time in meetings and consultations and substantially less time in direct contact with clients than health visitors do. While the figure of 50·9 per cent to represent the amount of time spent by health visitors in direct contact with patients may be slightly inflated, the lowest figure recorded in Table 4 (31 per cent; Study No. 29) is still higher than that recorded by either of the two studies of social workers.

The question of whether the proportion of time spent by health visitors on "less worthy" activities such as clerical duties should be reduced by delegation to ancillary workers has been the subject of much professional argument, and was listed as one of the purposes of the investigation in several of the studies included in this review (e.g. Nos. 3, 5, 7, 13, 24, 28). The answer to such a question is a matter for professional policy; it cannot be solely based on the findings of research, although research

Table 5

How the Health Visitor Spends her Time: Comparison with Studies of Social Workers

	% of total working time				
Name of Researcher	Client Contact	Travel	Meetings and Consultations	Clerical/ Admin	Other
Carver & Edwards[1]	30·0	16·0	14·0	30·0	10·0
Harris[2]	28·7	15·6	16·2[3]	25·6[4]	14·1[5]
Health Visitor Studies	50·9[6]	13·5[7]	6·9[8]	27·1[7]	

Notes to Table 5
1. Carver, V. & Edwards, J. L. (1972). Social Workers and their Workloads. National Institute for Social Work Training.
2. Harris, N. (1976). Management Services and Professional Staff. Management Services 20, 12, 34–37.
3. Formal meetings 7·9%; colleagues 8·3%.
4. Writing/dictating 20·8%; telephone 4·8%.
5. Supervision 6·7%; reading 3·5%; other 3·9%.
6. Mean of studies listed in Table 4.
7. Mean of studies listed in Table 2.
8. Mean of 7 studies which specified "meetings and consultation" as separate category (Nos. 1, 3, 5, 9, 19, 22, 33).

could and should be used to provide the factual data on which such a decision should be based. Although some of the studies listed above included some discussion of the question, the data presently available is not sufficiently detailed or precise to form a sound basis for decision, and further research designed for this specific purpose is needed. For example, the present data are limited to the *amount* of time allocated to the various activities; there are no data available about *sequence*. Yet it is likely that sequence of activities (i.e. the way in which the health visitor organises her day) will affect the amounts available. For example, if a health visitor decides that it is unwise to visit her families before 10 am, or at lunch time, or when mothers are fetching older children from school, or after 4.30 pm, the time available for visiting may be limited to four hours per day, and this amount of time will not be increased by the delegation of clerical tasks to other personnel.

The relative amounts of health visiting time spent on the various activities do, however, have important implications for policy decisions, for example, for the geographical deployment of services (travelling time) and for the training of health visitors. As Henderson (Study No. 19) remarks in relation to clerical duties:

"If it is really essential that health visitors spend so much of their time undertaking administrative duties, then greater emphasis must be placed on preparing them for this aspect of their work during their courses". (Henderson, 1977, Page 29).

CHAPTER 4

The Health Visitor's Clientele

Most accounts of the health visitor's clientele are based on the definition of a "primary patient" who is visited by the health visitor or attends some kind of clinic session. Records of "visits made" or "cases seen" are routinely collected and incorporated into national statistics as shown in Table 6.

The accuracy of these data is, however, questionable for several reasons:

1. A visit which includes more than one person may be recorded as more than one visit. Clark (1973) reports that:
   "in a survey . . . by Berkshire County Council in 1970 the number of visits made by health visitors during the survey period was recorded both by means of the survey forms (which recorded the total number of visits made), and by means of the normal statistical returns (which recorded the number of visits made to particular client groups). The number of visits recorded in the survey forms was 8,545, whereas the number recorded in the statistical returns was 15,441." (Clark, 1973, Page 42).
   The same phenomenon is also noted by Naidoo (Study No. 24).

2. The categories are not homogeneous nor mutually exclusive. Some categories specify individuals (e.g. children born in a particular year) while others specify households (e.g. tuberculous households). Clients are confused with problems (e.g. patients discharged from hospital, mentally ill).

3. Before 1971 the categories of client age-groups were not comprehensive. Cases of children under 5 years and persons over 65 years were recorded, but there was no category for clients in the intervening age-group.

4. There are other unexplained discrepancies. Hicks (1976) remarks:
   "I find some of the figures puzzling. For example 'Cases of children born that year' for 1971 reads 834·7 (thousands), whereas the population and vital statistics table in the same publication gives live births in 1971 as 783 (thousands). No doubt the statistician can explain the difference; there is a consistent difference in each year from 1965 to 1971." (Hicks, 1976, Page 264).

It is possible that this particular discrepancy is due to multiple recording for first and subsequent visits in the same year.

Table 6

The Health Visitor's Clientele: D.H.S.S. statistics

Service	Unit	1967	1969	1971[1]	1973	1975	1977
Health visiting							
Total cases attended	Thousands	5,213·4	5,103·3	5,158·5	5,047·9	4,662·6	4,671·1
	Per 1,000 population	97·8	94·9	95·4	92·8	85·7	86·0
Cases of[2]							
Children born that year	Thousands	969·3	921·5	924·4	817·6	784·2	725·6
Other children aged under 5	Thousands	3,112·4	2,962·7	2,826·8	2,401·3	2,139·2	1,996·9
Persons aged 65 or over	Thousands	379·0	418·2	518·1	660·1	627·9	662·6
	Per 1,000 population 65+	56·8	60·4	72·2	88·9	82·0	84·4
Mentally disordered persons	Thousands	29·1	32·6	34·0	59·4	59·2	48·8[3]
Tuberculosis households visited	Thousands	59·3	50·7	39·1	73·8	60·8	45·2[3]

Notes to Table 6
1. Because of a change of definition figures from 1972 are not comparable with earlier years.
2. A case appropriate to more than one heading is counted under each heading.
3. England and Wales only.

Source: Health and Personal Social Service statistics for England 1978 (1980) London, H.M.S.O.. Table 6·1 (Extract).

These problems are frequently repeated in the studies included in this review. Some of the researchers have attempted to avoid such problems by devising different category systems, but with limited success. For example, Marris (Study No. 22) uses a category system containing 37 precoded items from which respondents were expected to select the appropriate one; the categories incorporated both age groups and "problems" (e.g. T.B. pre-school age child). Since different researchers use different category systems, comparison of one study with another is not always possible.

Age Groups

The findings of 13 studies which are broadly comparable are shown in Table 7. These data refer only to home visits; clientele seen in clinic ses-

Table 7

The Health Visitor's Clientele: Percentage of Visits to Clients of Different Ages (13 studies)

Study No.	Name of Researcher	Date of Study	Children Under 5	Elderly	Other
1	Akester & MacPhail	1961	75·4	3·4	21·2
12	Fry *et al*	1963-64	82·0[1]	12·0	6·0
18	Graham[2]	1965	57·2	28·9	13·9
2	Allen & King	1965-66	78·8	4·0	17·2
9	Clow	1966	56·8[3]	23·4	19·8
16	Gilmore[4]	1967-68	48·8	36·2	15·0
16	Gilmore[5]	1967	68·6	24·6	6·8
16	Gilmore[6]	1967-68	67·0	25·0	7·0
3	Allen, King & Abbott[7]	1969	69·7	14·7	
8	Clark	1969	70·6	18·0	11·4
19	Henderson[8]	1975	58·0	9·0	33·0
29	Poulton	1976	80·0	20·0	
28	Potton	1977-78	79·0	21·0	
36	Wiseman	1978	54·0	20·0	26·0
32	Walworth-Bell[9]	1978	75·4	5·5	18·9

Notes to Table 7
1. Includes children up to 16 years.
2. Mid-point of reported range, therefore approximate only.
3. Includes expectant mothers.
4. First visits only.
5. All Brighton H.Vs, first visits 1967.
6. All visits, reported in Gilmore *et al* (1974).
7. Excludes 15·6% no reply visits.
8. % of people seen on visits, not % visits.
9. Figures based on the 69% of visits where primary patient was defined.

sions or elsewhere is not recorded here. The studies are arranged in chronological order to permit comparison over time. Table 8 which shows the findings of a single study (Study No. 22) is included because this study, while not comparable with any of the other studies because of its complicated category system and its idiosyncratic method of analysis, is important because of its detail and its large sample size.

It is clear from Tables 7 and 8 that the major component of the health visitor's clientele is families containing young children. The proportion of visits to the elderly, however, is very variable (range 3·4 per cent to 36·2 per cent) and has been the subject of considerable discussion. National annual statistics (Table 6) show a consistent gradual increase in both the absolute numbers and the proportion of visits to the elderly since 1965, and this increase is reflected in the studies reviewed here. The trend is usually explained in terms of the change in the age-structure of the general population which has brought an increasing awareness of the needs of the elderly which is reflected in official policies about priorities for care at both national and local level, and the policy of attachment to general practice (discussed in Chapter 13 of this review). Other factors, however, may be important in explaining the wide variation between individual studies. For example, it is not surprising that studies undertaken in Worthing (Study No. 18) and Brighton (Study No. 16) should record a higher proportion of visits to the elderly than studies undertaken elsewhere. The very low proportion of elderly clients reported in Studies

Table 8

The Health Visitor's Clientele: People Served by Health Visitors in Greater London

People Served	Percentage of total time spent	Percentage of total persons served
Unsupported mothers	2·4	3·6
Expectant mothers	2·6	4·7
Mothers and babies	13·6	31·2
Handicapped or T.B.	1·8	2·7
Mentally ill	1·2	1·7
Family unit	1·6	2·4
Organised group	1·6	2·2
Child pre- or at school	9·4	39·0
Teenager not at school	0·2	0·3
Young adult 20–39 years	1·9	3·8
Middle aged 40–59 years	0·6	1·1
Elderly 60+ years	1·5	2·1
Abortive call no-one	0·8	4·9
No-one	60·7	—

Source: Marris (1971) Table 5, Page 16 (Study No. 22).

No. 22 and No. 32 may be partly explained by the employment in London of specialist geriatric visitors who were not included in the study.

Socio-economic Background

The socio-economic background of the health visitor's clientele is very difficult to assess. The health visitor may not know the occupation of the head of the household in the families whom she visits and would probably be reluctant to ask merely for the purpose of a small-scale research study. Clark (Study No. 8) and Poulton (Study No. 29) attempted to record the data but found the data obtained so incomplete or imprecise that it was not included in the analysis. Jefferys (Study No. 20), Henderson (Study No. 19) and Naidoo (Study No. 25) appear to have been somewhat more successful, but Naidoo's data are meaningless without comparative information about the population from which the health visitor's clientele was drawn. Both Henderson and Naidoo, however, appear to show an over-representation of families at the lower end of the social scale. This is in contrast to the findings of Jefferys (Study No. 20) who specifically remarks that her findings "suggest that health visitors, unlike most other social welfare staff, visited a fairly representative social cross-section".

Henderson further categorises the clients seen by health visitors in her survey as "independent" (including retired if not receiving supplementary benefit), or "dependent" (receiving Family Income Supplement or Supplementary Benefit); 79 per cent of clients were categorised as "independent", 21 per cent as "dependent". Henderson comments "the dependent group seems high. They may well be a more obviously needy group". (Henderson 1977, Page 59).

Poulton (Study No. 29) in her sample of 511 families visited by health visitors in her study in Wandsworth and East Merton, was unable to analyse her data on social class because of their ambiguity, but reported that 63·4 per cent of families appeared to be self-supporting. 23 per cent of her sample received supplementary benefit, 21·7 per cent had poor accommodation, 11 per cent an unsatisfactory water supply and 14·6 per cent inadequate heating (Poulton 1977, Page 52).

The samples are too small and the methodological inadequacies far too great for conclusions to be drawn from these data, but it might tentatively be suggested that this discrepancy between the study undertaken in 1961 (Jefferys) and the three studies undertaken in 1975–76 (Henderson, Naidoo, and Poulton) reflects the shift of emphasis away from "routine visiting" to "crisis work" which has been widely reported by health visitors but supported only by anecdotal evidence.

Problem Group

In several studies clients are categorised according to some kind of "problem" label (e.g. mentally ill, handicapped person). Since these categories are usually included with the more obvious age-group categories the proportion of clients within them is usually very small (often less than one per cent), and the category systems themselves so varied that comparisons are impossible. One such category, however—"unsupported mothers"—is used by several studies which can therefore be compared: Henderson, (Study No. 19) reported that 11 per cent of visits were to one-parent families, Poulton (Study No. 29) 17·3 per cent, and Wiseman (Study No. 3) 2 per cent, while Marris (Study No. 22) reported that 4·4 per cent of "persons served" on home visits and 3·6 per cent of all "persons served" were unsupported mothers.

Four studies (Nos. 4, 16, 17, 20) asked respondents to record the existence of health or social problems in the families they visited. The prevalence of health problems reported ranged from 7·7 per cent to 38 per cent, and the prevalence of social problems from 6·7 per cent to 100 per cent. Interpretation of these data is extremely difficult. In addition to the problems of choice of categories (which vary from study to study and are rarely comprehensive), and comparison between the study population and the general population in a particular area, it is important to appreciate that the figures relate to health visitors' perception of problems and not to the existence of problems as established by any objective criteria. There are in fact wide differences in reporting between different kinds of staff and different health visitors. Jefferys specifically considers this problem (Jefferys 1965, Pages 70–74) and similar discrepancies are also noted by Gilmore et al (Gilmore et al, 1974, Page 131). The extent to which problems are perceived and reported is clearly related to the training and field of interest of the reporter.

Clients in Contact with Other Agencies

Clark (1973) suggested that:

"A considerable part of the value of the health visitor in the detection of health and social needs and the prevention of distress and family breakdown is due to the fact that she visits a great many families whom no-one else visits". (Clark, 1973, Page 50).

The proportion of visits in which the health visitor was thought to be the only agency visiting is shown in Table 9. All of these studies also include details of the other agencies involved but the categories used vary too widely for comparison and these data are, therefore, not included in the Table. For example, Clark (Study No. 8) reported that in 27·6 per cent of households visited a general practitioner was known to be visiting, in 7·6 per cent a district nurse was visiting, in 4·1 per cent a social worker from the Children's Department and in 5·0 per cent a social worker from the Welfare Department (this study was undertaken before the inception of integrated Social Services Departments). Poulton (Study No. 29) reported that 3 per cent of her sample were also visited by a district nurse, 21 per cent by a social worker, 6·5 per cent by a home help, and

Table 9

*The Health Visitor's Clientele: Proportion in which the Health Visitor
was the Only Agency in Contact (4 studies)*

Study No.	Name of Researcher	Percentage of families/visits in which the health visitor was thought to be the only agency.
1	Akester and MacPhail	70
20	Jefferys	85
8	Clark	60
19	Henderson	64

6·5 per cent by other social services. It should be appreciated, however, that health visitors do not always know when another agency is visiting a family; Jefferys (Study No. 20) reported that in 75 instances where other social welfare workers in the same study were known to have recently visited the families visited by the health visitors, in 40 per cent of cases the health visitor had no knowledge of the other worker.

Discussion

In theory, at least, the health visitor is unique among health and social welfare workers in her ability to determine her own clientele by selection from the population at large. This is because she is able to make contact with clients on her own initiative without the necessity for a specific request for help. The ability and indeed the responsibility to do so is considered essential to the exercise of her function in the prevention of ill health. In theory differences in health visiting clientele at different times and in different areas should merely reflect differences in the overall population structure.

In practice, however, the health visitor has traditionally drawn her clientele from the families with young children whom she has a statutory responsibility to visit. To this clientele the policy of attachment of health visitors to general practices and the development of primary health care teams has added clients referred by the general practitioner and other members of the team, and also the opportunity (for example if the practice has an age-sex register or some other "register" of defined groups within the practice population) for the health visitor herself to identify and seek out other individuals. She may also accept referrals from other health agencies (e.g. hospitals), social service agencies, voluntary organisations, friends, relatives of clients, or accept clients who ask directly for her help.

It is not at all easy to relate the health visitor's reported clientele to her potential clientele defined either in terms of the population as a whole, or in terms of a general practice population (the health visitor's caseload as defined by the policy of attachment to general practice), or in terms of the "vulnerable groups" implied by official prescriptions of the health visitor's role (e.g. C.E.T.H.V. 1969).

This task was, however, the main aim of Wiseman's study (Study No. 36). Wiseman identified 26 "care groups" and used a variety of data sources (for example the 1971 census, the A.H.A. epidemiology unit statistics, the sector "at risk" register) to estimate the number of people in each care group existing in her study area (one sector of a health district). She then asked her health visitor respondents to record their visits, allocating each client to one or more of the "care groups", over a period of nine weeks. She also interviewed nurse managers and asked them to determine an upper (ideal) level and a lower (minimum) level of health visiting contact for clients in each care group. The three "profiles" were then compared and the discrepancies between them noted and discussed.

Walworth-Bell (Study No. 29) similarly attempted to match "needs" for health visiting with records of visits to two particular client groups—new babies and elderly people (over 75 years). The population in each client group was estimated from birth notifications and Family Practitioner Committee records, and the number of visits recorded by health visitors was compared with an arbitrary ideal. The ideal for the new birth group was two visits, plus two more visits if the baby was of low birth weight, plus four more visits if the mother was unmarried; the ideal for the elderly group was one visit per year. For the new birth group the actual number of visits was very near to the calculated ideal, (92·1 per cent), but for the elderly group the discrepancy was much larger and differed both between and within the two health districts (66·1 per cent in Greenwich, 16·4 per cent in Bexley). A similar attempt in the City of Leicester (Study No. 7) in which the visiting "standard" was set by the M.O.H., showed even larger discrepancies, especially for the elderly.

White (Study No. 34) attempted to calculate staffing requirements on the basis of an "ideal" visiting requirement determined from a questionnaire completed by health visitors and an estimated visit duration based on the durations recorded in other studies, but did not compare the ideal with the actual records of visits. From an analysis of the health visitors' caseloads, however, she found that "the total number of elderly persons known to the health visitors was ... approximately, one sixth of the total number of those over 65 years".

Estimates of the population of children under five years and of elderly people in a given area are not too difficult to calculate, and comparison between these figures and the numbers of visits recorded by health visitors could offer health authorities a useful, if somewhat crude, measure of the "coverage" provided by their health visiting services. For example, in Berkshire (unpublished data) comparison between the health visiting statistics and the child population for the year 1976 showed that health visitors actually visited only 78 per cent of the population whom they have a statutory obligation to visit (number of cases of children under five years seen by health visitors 43,160; estimated population of children under five years 55,200). A discrepancy of this kind might offer a much more cogent indicator of the need for more health visitors in an area than the currently used "norms" or "recommended health visitor: population ratios".

Gilmore (Study No. 16) and Gilmore *et al* (Study No. 17) were specifically concerned with the work of a primary health care team within practices whose populations could be specified in detail. Gilmore (1970) reported that in the practice studied in Brighton, the two health visitors visited between them 26 per cent of the total practice population; in this study, however, a high proportion of the visits (43 per cent of first visits) were initiated by the general practitioner. Although Gilmore *et al* (1974) included in their report an extensive discussion of the utilisation of practice resources such as the age-sex register, no figure comparable with the earlier study's 26 per cent is reported.

With potentially such an unlimited clientele to be served by very limited health visiting resources, selection is inevitable. The criteria on which such selection is made are rarely specified. They must be assumed to include differences in population structure (e.g. the proportion of young children or elderly persons in the local population), administrative policies set by employing authorities, and the pressure of referrals. In addition, since the final decision about who to visit is made by the individual health visitor, the choice must be coloured by individual priorities reflecting individual interests and aptitudes.

CHAPTER 5

The Pattern of Home Visits

Home visits were shown in Chapter 3 to account for between a quarter and a third of the health visitor's time; the proportion ranged from 17·4 per cent to 58·1 per cent. Compared with the other broad categories of activity, home visiting is, in terms of the time devoted to it, the most important constituent of health visiting activity. Health visitors themselves would probably regard it as their most important activity for other reasons over and above the proportion of time allocated to it, and this emphasis is reflected in the number of studies and the amount of data reported which focus primarily or exclusively on the health visitor's home visits.

Description of the pattern of home visits should present fewer methodological difficulties than the description of some other aspects of the health visitor's work because each visit constitutes a single discrete episode; each visit is a single unit which can be allocated to a single cell in a category system, and the total recorded is likely to be a valid base for calculating proportions. Two major sources of confusion remain, however. The first is the confusion between the number of visits and the number of persons visited, i.e. a single visit may be counted as a visit to two persons and this may appear in some reports as two visits; this problem was discussed in Chapter 4. The second is the confusion between effective and "ineffective" or "no reply" visits; in the total reported, "ineffective" visits are sometimes included, sometimes excluded, and whether they are included or not is often not specified.

The overall proportion of time devoted to home visiting conceals considerable variation in the number of visits made in a day or week and in the length of the individual visits. The number of visits made by health visitors on average during a day or during a week is shown in Table 10. It is important to appreciate that "average" in this sense means "statistical mean" and not "typical"; daily figures in particular are distorted by whether the day includes, for example, a clinic session, which would be expected to take up a large proportion of a particular day. It is apparent that some of the figures are distorted by the confusion between "visits" and "visits to a person" which has already been mentioned; this probably explains some of the high figures recorded.

The number of visits made in a day or in a week must be related to the duration of visits. The average duration of visits reported by nine studies is shown in Table 11. A further five studies (Nos. 1, 8, 23, 25, 32) report

Table 10

*Number of Visits Made by a Health Visitor in an Average Day or an
Average Week (13 studies)*

Study No.	Name of Researcher	Date of Study	Number of Visits per Day	Number of Visits per Week
23	Ministry of Health	1955	Not Specified	48
1	Akester and MacPhail	1961	Not Specified	30
18	Graham	1965	9·6[1]	Not Specified
21	Loveland[2]	1968	a) 5·45; b) 6·44	Not Specified
16	Gilmore[3]	1967–68	Not Specified	a) 9·6; b) 22·4
14	Gettings	1967–68	7	Not Specified
7	City of Leicester	1968–69	Not Specified	29[6]
5	Atkinson	1970	Not Specified	45
8	Clark	1969	Not Specified	30
33	Watson	1975	Not Specified	a) 20; b) 30[4]
29	Poulton	1976	5	Not Specified
28	Potton	1977	5·6	28·2
32	Walworth-Bell	1978	7·3[5]	

Notes to Table 10
1. Mid-point of reported range 6·6–12·6.
2. a) Merton; b) Wiltshire. Successful visits only included.
3. a) Study of two health visitors; a) H.V.I; b) H.V.II.
4. a) H.V. who spent least time of visiting; b) H.V. who spent most time visiting; both figures are for period of four consecutive days.
5. 3·6 per session.
6. 29 "effective" visits plus 6 "no reply" visits; figures calculated from monthly totals divided by 4.

the relative frequency of visits of different durations. For example, Clark (Study No. 8) reported that 28·4 per cent of visits lasted less than 15 minutes, and 50·9 per cent lasted between 15 and 29 minutes, 16·9 per cent lasted between 30 and 59 minutes, and 3·4 per cent lasted longer than an hour; she also analysed in detail the characteristics of very short (less than 15 minutes) and very long (longer than 1 hour) visits.

Wilkes and Nimmo (Study No. 35), however, reported that:

"The surveys produced no evidence that average visit times depend on the daily workload, and for example the average could be the same when only 5 calls were made in a day as when 18 were made. Nor did average times decrease when part of the day was taken up with clinic sessions or other special activities, although the number of calls made on such days were on average much less than on days devoted primarily to visiting. Differences existed in the average length of time individual health visitors devoted per visit; one took much longer on visits than the others while another generally made shorter visits irrespective of the age group concerned".

Table 11

Average Duration of Home Visits (9 studies)

Study No.	Name of Researcher	Average duration of visit (minutes)
23	Ministry of Health	15
18	Graham	24[1]
13	Gallaher *et al*	19
34	White	13
28	Potton	18·5
33	Watson	17
29	Poulton	24
7	City of Leicester	25[2]
37	Young	22[3]

Notes to Table 11
1. Calculated from reported range of 2·3 to 2·7 visits per hour.
2. The mean duration of visits to children was 22 minutes, and to elderly persons 28 minutes; the mean duration of "unscheduled street stops" was nine minutes.
3. "Obstetric" visit 13 minutes; "paediatric" visit 18 minutes; "geriatric" visit 38 minutes; "infectious diseases" visit 18 minutes.

Watson (Study No. 33) and Gilmore *et al* (Study No. 17) also reported evidence of wide variation between individual health visitors.

A further important source of variation in the duration of visits is the type of visit. The duration of visits to clients of different ages and with different kinds of problems is reported in studies Nos. 9, 17, 28, 29, 33 and 35. Clark (Study No. 8) found that the length of visit varied with the clientele, the purpose of the visit, and the source of the visit.

Manipulation of the three factors of number of visits, duration of visits and proportion of time allocated to visiting, particularly when the findings of one study on one factor are extrapolated to other studies which considered different factors, produces very misleading results which may lead to spurious conclusions. For example, Hicks (1976) writes of Study No. 8: "This research describes what health visitors in Berkshire did in no more than 15 per cent of their working time, crediting 15 minutes devoted to each of 26 domiciliary visits in a week". In fact neither the proportion of time allocated to visiting nor the average duration of visits was reported in this study.

Two studies (No. 13 and No. 37) used the mean duration of visits to set "performance targets". Gallaher *et al* (Study No. 13) reported the findings of a second survey undertaken after the performance targets were implemented; they report that the number of visits recorded increased from 30,889 in 1967 (before performance targets) to 42,518 in 1968 (after performance targets), and to 44,920 in 1969, without any reduction in the length of visits, or in the number of clinic or school sessions. The variability in the duration of visits and the general methodological problems discussed in Chapter 2 must raise questions about the validity and reliability of these data and the interpretation to be placed on the findings; but a more serious question is the use of such quantitative data to draw conclusions about quality of performance, by using the ratios as "a measure of overall nursing performance and performance trends" (Young, 1971, Page 161).

The proportion of ineffective or "no access" visits reported in eight studies is shown in Table 12. In addition to these studies which expressed their findings as a percentage of all visits, three studies reported the proportion of total time spent on "ineffective" visits. Henderson (Study No. 19) reported that 1 per cent of the total time was spent on "no reply" visits; the City of Leicester (Study No. 7) reported 1·4 per cent. Marris (Study No. 22) reported that "Abortive calls occupied between 4 and 5 per cent of health visitors' domiciliary visiting time. (It should be re-iterated that as a proportion of all their time abortive calls amounted to less than 1 per cent). No doubt health visitors tried to waste as few minutes as possible on such unproductive work and the average of only four minutes per call is low". (Marris, 1971, Page 20).

Potton (Study No. 28) attempted to relate the proportion of "no reply" visits to the time of day. He found that the vast majority of visits (86·7 per cent) were made between 10 am and 4 pm, with the hour between 11 am and 12 noon being the most popular time (26·4 per cent); 57·4 per cent were made before 1 pm. The proportion of "no reply" visits varied from 4 per cent among the small number of visits made before 10 am and after 6 pm (these visits were made by special arrangement) to 24·4 per cent of the visits made between 3 pm and 4 pm when presumably many mothers would be out collecting children from school. The main reason

Table 12

Proportion of "Ineffective" or "No reply" Visits (8 studies)

Study No.	Name of Researcher	Location of Study	Percentage of all visits recorded as "ineffective" or "no reply"
23	Ministry of Health a) cities	National	17
	b) counties	Sample	6
1	Akester and MacPhail	Leeds	16·2
9	Clow	Croydon	11·4
3	Allen, King and Abbott	Hertfordshire	15·6
37	Young	Bolton	25
19	Henderson	Hampshire	9
28	Potton	Kent	18·6
32	Walworth-Bell	Greenwich and Bexley	18·8

for this apparently high proportion of unproductive activity is that health visitors, unlike other health and social welfare workers, may visit on their own initiative, without need for a referral, without informing the client that they are coming, and only rarely by appointment. It is known that some health visitors do, in fact, work at least partly by appointment but this is not recorded in any of the research studies. A specific study of "no access" visits, not included in this review, has been reported by Johnson *et al.* (1978).

The initiation or source of the home visit is very complex and difficult to categorise and analyse.

As Akester and MacPhail (Study No. 1) remark:

"To discover who or what prompts a visit may be simple, as in notification of birth, for example. Very often, however, several factors are involved and it proves difficult to describe the initiation of the visit in a neat and tidy manner suitable for tabulation. Thus, a health visitor may enquire after the well-being of a family to be told by the neighbour that some sort of crisis has arisen. As happens occasionally, several agencies may phone the health visitor simultaneously about a family already known to her. The initiating sources in one case of our sample of 1,000 included the family doctor, the hospital, the midwife, and a relative, all of whom contacted the health visitor urgently for a very difficult situation requiring, one might say, a 'social fire brigade'. Again, a health visitor may decide, on her own initiative, to contact a family brought to her notice long before the police, the N.S.P.C.C. or by the health inspector". (Akester and MacPhail, 1961, Page 21).

Initiation or source is closely linked with purpose and presenting problem, and several studies (e.g. Nos. 3, 5, 9, 29) include all three dimensions within a single category which is usually labelled "Type of Visit". The sources of home visits reported by eight studies are shown in Table 13.

Clark (Study No. 8) following Akester and MacPhail (Study No. 1) distinguished between "planned" and "unintended" visits. Akester and MacPhail (1961) remarked:

"We have always known that health visitors on their rounds discover or uncover many previously unknown situations calling for action. We also know that most of this goes unrecorded". (Akester and MacPhail, 1961, Page 21).

They found that 31·4 per cent of all visits were "picked up" in this way, and stressed the importance of this aspect of the health visitor's work. Clark recorded a lower proportion (19 per cent), but noted that these visits took up a considerable amount of time (56 per cent of them lasted longer than 15 minutes); they did not differ significantly in terms of clientele, purpose, initiation or length from planned visits. Henderson (1977) did not record the proportion of all visits, but reported that 2 per cent of total time was spent on "impulse visits" (compared with 23 per cent on all visits); in the City of Leicester (Study No. 7) the proportion was 0·5 per cent.

Table 13
Source/Initiation of Home Visits (8 studies)

Study No.	Name of Researcher	Percentage of visits initiated by:						
		H.V.	Client	G.P.	Primary Health Care Team	Hospital	Other	Unspecified/ Not Known
23	Ministry of Health	87	6	Not Specified	Not Specified	Not Specified	7	—
3	Allen, King & Abbott[1]	91.9	5.4	1.8	Not Specified	Not Specified	0.9	—
8	Clark	63.5	13.6	7.3	1.2	1.1	12.3[2]	1.0
25	Naidoo	60.6	33.9	Not Specified	Not Specified	Not Specified	Not Specified	—
16	Gilmore[3]	Not Specified	18.7	43.3	7.9	4.9	25.1[4]	0.1
17	Gilmore et al[5]	59.3[6]	6.0	17.3	17.3	Not Specified	17.0	—
32	Walworth-Bell	74.5	13	4	Not Specified	6.5	Not Specified	0.4
36	Wiseman	71		Not Specified	Not Specified	Not Specified	Not Specified	—

Notes to Table 13
1. Visits to children only.
2. Includes "other nursing staff" 1.4%; M.O.H. 1.8%; Welfare Dept. 0.6%; Children's Dept. 0.3%; voluntary agency 0.2%; chance meeting 5.8%.
3. First visits only.
4. Includes 8.8% "birth notifications"; 3.4% practice records.
5. Mean of three centres.
6. "Planned revisits".

The purpose or reason for the visit is even more difficult to categorise and analyse than the source. As Clark (1973) remarks:

"Unlike the nurse she does not visit in order to provide a clearly defined clinical service; unlike the social worker she does not visit in order to deal with a known problem . . . It is not always easy to isolate the purpose of the visit from the initiator of the visit (e.g. the request of a GP to visit a family) and from what actually happened during the course of the visit". (Clark, 1973, Page 44).

Clark reported that in her study the purpose of the visit was the only question which was not pre-coded, and that in spite of two pilot studies it was found necessary to change the category system for the data of the main study. The category systems used by various researchers vary so widely that no two studies are comparable; the findings of individual studies must, therefore, be looked at separately. Studies No. 3, 8, 17, 25 and 32 report "Reason" or "Purpose" of visits; in Studies No. 5, 9, 19, 28 and 29, the purpose is included in the categorisation of "Type of Visit".

Discussion

The health visitor herself has final control over whom she visits, how much time she spends on each visit, and what action she takes during the visit and subsequently; she is responsible for determining her own priorities and organising her own work. It is likely, therefore, that the data presented in this chapter conceal considerable variability in the pattern of work recorded and this needs to be taken into account in interpreting the various findings. Further research is needed to find the extent and causes of variation, but the present data do provide some clues.

For example, Clark (Study No. 8) reported statistically significant differences between visits recorded by health visitors of different ages and different types of training. The differences were differences of clientele, sources of visits, and recorded purposes as well as content. Marris (Study No. 22) found similar differences which he attributed to geographical factors, but which could also be attributed to the factors identified by Clark. Henderson (Study No. 19) also found differences in the purpose and orientation of visits which she attributed to the same factors. She reported:

"Three factors stand out as being associated with differences in visiting patterns. These were:
1. whether the H.V. course was completed under the old or new syllabus;
2. how long the H.V. had been in full-time practice;
3. whether the workload was geographically or G.P. based." (Henderson, 1977, Page 42).

The clinical freedom which permits such individual variability is a facet of health visiting which is highly valued by health visitors and jealously guarded. The use of performance targets as suggested by Gallaher *et al* (Study No. 13) and Young (Study No. 37) is not likely to be welcomed. Both authors in fact report a certain resistance to their implementation. There is no evidence to suggest that the use of such quantitative controls will improve quality of performance. It is, however, perhaps more reasonable to suggest that nationally agreed policies and priorities, provided that they incorporate professional consultation and agreement, should be reflected in individual practice. Before this can be achieved, however, much more needs to be known about the criteria on which health visitors determine their priorities, the operational constraints and other factors which affect the way in which they plan their work, and the objectives which they set for themselves in their professional practice.

CHAPTER 6

Work in Clinics

In Chapter 3 of this review it was shown that work in clinics accounted for approximately 15 per cent of the health visitor's working time. The range reported by the various studies was 2·1 per cent to 29·2 per cent. This chapter attempts to draw together what is reported about this part of health visiting activity.

Comparisons between studies are again impeded by the use of different category systems. Some studies specify "clinic", others use the term "sessions" which may include other "group" activities such as ante-natal classes. Some studies (e.g. Nos. 8, 25, 32, 33 and 36) specifically exclude work in clinics from their considerations. Other studies (e.g. many of those listed in Table 2) report only in broad outline. For these reasons the data included in this chapter are discussed mainly in terms of individual studies.

The study which gives probably the greatest detail about the health visitor's work in clinics is that of Marris (Study No. 22). Marris found that time spent in clinics accounted for 71 minutes of an average working day, or 14 per cent of health visitors' time, including the time spent in preparation and clearing up. The clinics were mainly child health sessions, but the data also include school clinics and pre- and post-natal clinics.

Marris presents his data in terms of the people served, the activities or "techniques" recorded, and the time allocated to each, expressed as a percentage of total recording time and as "time per person" or "time per activity". The "persons served" and the "time per person" during clinics are shown in Table 14. Marris reports:

"Half their clinic time was spent at child welfare clinics and at these each activity took 6 minutes, so that as a proportion of all activities the services to people at child welfare clinics represented 16 per cent of the total. Activities at school clinics were extremely short—only 3 minutes each—so that although they occupied little more than 1 per cent of health visitor's time the speed with which people were seen meant that such activities represented 6 per cent of the total. (Marris, 1971, Page 29).

"It was at clinics that health visitors most often served members of the public; excluding the occasions when health visitors were not serving any individual, for instance when travelling or at meals doing general administrative work, 42 per cent of the acts of service to individuals took place during clinics. This compares with 31 per cent of acts of service which took place during

45

Table 14

People Served at Clinics in Greater London

	Time Spent		People Served
	Proportion	Average	Proportion
Total	145,806 minutes 100%	7 minutes per person	22,274 people 100%
People	%	minutes	%
Unsupported expectant mother	0·6	12	0·3
Unsupported mother 1st year after confinement	1·4	9	1·1
Unsupported mother later	0·5	9	0·4
Expectant mother 1st child	2·9	9	2·1
Expectant mother 2nd or subsequent child	3·0	8	2·5
Mother and baby after 1st confinement	21·5	7	21·2
Mother and baby after 2nd confinement	16·8	6	18·1
Handicapped or chronically ill	1·0	12	0·6
T.B.	0·1	...	0·1
Mentally ill	0·5	9	0·4
Family unit	0·2	...	0·2
School or play group	0·0	...	0·0
Child-minder	0·4	7	0·4
Baby not with mother	1·0	7	0·9
Child not at school	13·2	6	15·5
Girl 5–14 or at school	5·3	3	12·1
Boy 5–14 or at school	5·6	3	12·3
Female 15–19	0·1	...	0·1
Female 20–39	1·9	8	1·6
Female 40–59	0·6	9	0·4
Female 60–69	0·4	...	0·2
Female 70+	0·3	...	0·2
Male 15–19	0·0	...	0·0
Male 20–39	0·1	...	0·1
Male 40–59	0·0	...	0·0
Male 60–69	0·1	...	0·0
Male 70+	0·2	...	0·1
Abortive call	—	—	—
No-one	22·1	15	9·4

Source: Marris (1971) Table 7, Page 20.

Notes to Table 14: 0·0 = less than 0·05   — = none   ... = insufficient data

The 22·1% allocated to "no-one" represents the time spent preparing for a clinic or clearing away after it and the intervals between patients.

domiciliary visiting. But serving people at clinic sessions did not take health visitors as long: an average of only 7 minutes per person compared with 12 minutes during domiciliary visiting. Because of this the proportion of all the time devoted to individuals was less during clinic sessions than during domiciliary visiting. Specifically: of all the time spent serving individual people, 44 per cent was occupied in domiciliary visiting and 28 per cent in clinic sessions. The relative importance of clinic work and domiciliary work, therefore, changes according to whether we are considering the number of people served, or the time taken in serving them". (Marris, 1971, Page 20).

Marris further notes that there were several instances, where health visitors were holding large scale clinics, of health visitors attending to more than 100 people during the course of a day or half a day's work. (Perhaps this highlights the difficulty of asking health visitors to record their own activities and clientele).

Although he records in detail the "techniques" used with different people and in different boroughs, Marris unfortunately does not compare the "techniques" of clinic work with those of home visits; such a comparison would have been permitted by the raw data, and might have been useful.

Nimmo undertook two specific studies of child health clinics (Studies No. 26 and 27). He obtained data by means of a "survey card" given to each mother on arrival at clinics; the card included details of the children (up to three children per card), whether this was the first clinic attendance, the mode of travel to the clinic, the arrival time and the consultation time, and the health visitor's action in respect of each child. He found that the children were mainly very young (88 per cent aged twelve months or younger), and that 55 per cent saw the health visitor only (i.e. not the doctor). The duration of the consultations was very short—$3 \cdot 3$ minutes at Seaton clinic, $6 \cdot 7$ minutes at Denburn. What the health visitor actually did was not reported.

Other researchers report their findings in much less detail. The Jameson Report (Study No. 23) found that the average clinic lasted $2 \cdot 4$ hours: two thirds of clinics lasted between $2\frac{1}{2}$ and $3\frac{1}{2}$ hours, one third lasted longer than $3\frac{1}{2}$ hours. Poulton (Study No. 27) reported that the average time per clinic session was just under one hour. Gilmore et al (Study No. 17) reported that the average time per day spent by health visitors in clinics and group health education (the two activities were not specified separately) as recorded over two periods of ten days, was 68 minutes in Centre A, 100 minutes in Centre B and 35 minutes in Centre C.

The great majority of clinics recorded are child health clinics. Poulton records the proportion as $88 \cdot 9$ per cent, including toddlers clinics, and the amount of time spent on them as $83 \cdot 7$ per cent of the total time spent in clinic sessions. Atkinson (Study No. 5) reported that child health, immunisation, and hearing screening clinic sessions taken together constituted $14 \cdot 5$ per cent of total time, when the time taken for all clinic ses-

47

sions together constituted 17·4 per cent of total time. Allen, King and Abbot (Study No. 3) reported that L.H.A. and G.P. child health sessions and immunisation sessions together constituted 54·5 per cent of all sessions, school health sessions constituted 21 per cent, health education 10·3 per cent, with the remaining 23·2 per cent divided between hospital liason (2·6 per cent), other G.P. sessions (4·4 per cent), meetings (13·3 per cent), case conferences (1·5 per cent) and others (1·6 per cent).

Only Poulton (Study No. 29) and Allen, King and Abbott (Study No. 3) report the place where clinic sessions were held. Poulton reports that 6·4 per cent of child health sessions took place in G.P. surgeries; Allen, King and Abbott report that 10·4 per cent of all health visitor sessions were spent "working with general practitioners".

Marris' account of the work undertaken in clinics has already been discussed. Compared with the 22·1 per cent of the total clinic time spent in preparation, clearing, and pausing between client contacts reported by Marris, Clow (Study No. 9) reported that health visitors spent approximately 47 minutes per week on these activities (mean of attached and non-attached health visitors). Nimmo (Study No. 26) noted that the total time for these activities (105 minutes) was almost as long as the clinic session itself; the largest single item was record keeping (23 minutes) followed by clinic preparation (22 minutes) and tidying up (19 minutes).

Allen, King and Abbott sought, by means of questionnaires, further information about health visitors' activities in clinics. They found that 40 per cent of health visitors prepared clinics, 8 per cent routinely weighed babies, 56 per cent ordered stock, 41 per cent were responsible for laundry, and 83 per cent put up health education displays. Only 51 per cent of health visitors had an interviewing room available; 39 per cent of clinic consultations took place in the main hall, 37 per cent in a separate room of the clinic, 21 per cent in either the main hall or a separate room, and 3 per cent elsewhere.

Discussion

The information available about the activities of health visitors in clinic sessions is sparse. Statistics are routinely collected of the numbers of children of various ages seen by health visitors and by clinic doctors during clinic sessions. The large numbers of clients seen during a clinic session is an indication of the pace of activity in the clinic setting which would probably prevent accurate self-recorded data being obtained. The clinic is, however, a public setting where observational methods would be relatively easy to use to obtain accurate data, both about clientele and about health visitor activity.

CHAPTER 7

Work in Schools and Health Education in Groups

The time allocated by health visitors to work in schools as reported in the studies included in this review was very small. The proportions shown by the 14 studies which listed school work among the activities recorded (Table 15) ranged from 0·8 per cent to 9·6 per cent. Two studies, however, (Study No. 15 and Study No. 31) concentrate primarily on school work.

Table 15

Time Spent on School Work (14 studies)

Study No.	Name of Researcher	Percentage of total time spent on school work
3	Allen, King and Abbott	5·4
4	Ambler *et al*	0·8
5	Atkinson	9·1
7	City of Leicester	3·0
9	Clow	3·9
13	Gallaher *et al*	8·0[1]
18	Graham	6·0[2]
19	Henderson	1·0
22	Marris	1·6
24	Morris	6·56
31	Thurmott	9·6
33	Watson	1·0
34	White	2·6

Notes to Table 15
1. Includes teaching.
2. Mid-point of reported range 5%–7%.

Some indication of the activities undertaken during this time is given in Table 16. It is important to appreciate, however, that the four studies included are not directly comparable because their category systems differ slightly, and Gettings' account (Study No. 15) is of activities undertaken in an authority which has a separate specialist school nursing service.

Table 16
Activities Undertaken in School Work (4 studies)

Activity	Percentage of time on school work	Percentage of total time			
	Gettings (Study No. 15)	Atkinson (Study No. 5)	Thurmott (Study No. 31)	Morris (Study No. 24)	
Home follow up	5·8	1·0	1·26	0·35	
Hygiene inspection	—	2·1[1]	1·14	0·49	
Medical examination	—	1·3	3·55	1·83	
Immunisation	—	0·2	Not specified	0·22	
Vision testing	—	1·3[2]	0·37	0·51	
Audiometric testing	—	0·9	Not specified	Not specified	
Health education/teaching	57·8	0·6	0·86	Not specified	
Consultation/teacher liaison	17·8	0·7	Not specified	1·67	
Clerical	—	1·0	1·05	0·41	
Counselling	7·1			0·58	
Treatment sessions	—	Not specified	0·02	0·05	
Other	11·3[5]	Not specified	1·34[3]	0·15[4]	
Total allocated to schoolwork	100·0	9·1	9·6	6·56	

Notes to Table 16
1. Includes foot inspection 0·3%; scabies inspection 0·1%.
2. Includes colour testing 0·2%.
3. Includes travel 0·95%; developmental testing and screening 0·03%; pre-medical inspections 0·002%.
4. Children seen as result of liaison.
5. Travel associated with school work.

50

Allen, King and Abbot (Study No. 3) reported that:

"In duties relating to medical examinations, in primary schools 95 per cent of health visitors were involved and 72 per cent in relation to secondary schools. Some of the duties were delegated to the health visitors' assistants; 20 per cent of health visitors delegated their work fully to the assistants, 30 per cent of health visitors chose to carry out the duties with an assistant ... At the time of the survey 73 per cent of health visitors were involved in vision testing in schools with or without assistance ... Hygiene inspections were carried out by 33 per cent of health visitors working on their own, 26 per cent worked with an assistant, and 37 per cent of health visitors chose to delegate this duty to their assistants ... 37 per cent of health visitors involved in medical examinations transcribed details from parents' questionnaires on to the medical records of the school ... Only 20 per cent of health visitors were concerned with minor ailment clinics which were mainly used for the treatment of verrucae. The assistant carried out treatment in 80 per cent of the clinics" (Allen, King and Abbot, 1969, Page 12).

The Leverhulme Health Education Project found that only nine of 120 health visitor respondents in Nottinghamshire in 1977 had spent time on school medical work during the study week, but 66 (55 per cent) were involved in teaching in schools, and 41 (33 per cent) had counselled one or more school-children during the previous year. (Perkins, 1978).

Thurmott (Study No. 28) found that the health visitor on average served four schools and 1,136 pupils. Access to information was limited. One in three health visitors had lists of children plus their general practitioners; two in five had lists of the children without their G.P.'s; three in five had neither. (N.B. multiple answers because each H.V. had four schools). The facilities in schools varied greatly; 13 out of 20 health visitors in 16 out of 40 schools did not have medical rooms.

Less is known about the way in which the health visitor's school health function is exercised than about almost any other health visiting activity (with the possible exception of group health education). The overall time reported as devoted to this part of her work is very small and few details are reported. Further research is clearly needed. A study of the school health service in 12 primary schools in London is currently being undertaken by Thurmott.

Discussion

Even less is reported in the studies reviewed about the health visitor's teaching activities with groups. Most studies which record "health education to groups" do not distinguish between schools and other groups. Such information as is available from 10 studies is shown in Table 17.

It should be appreciated that the figures are distorted downwards because they represent an average based on all health visitors in the sample whereas it is known that many health visitors do not undertake group teaching at all. For example, Allen, King and Abbott (Study No. 3) reported that 25 per cent of their health visitors did no group

Table 17

Health Teaching with Groups: Time as a Percentage of Total Time Recorded
(10 studies)

Study No.	Name of Researcher	Percentage of total time
1	Akester and MacPhail	0·9
3	Allen, King and Abbott	2·6
4	Ambler *et al*	1·6
5	Atkinson	2·1
9	Clow	1·8
18	Graham	2·8[1]
19	Henderson—1% mothers	
	1% schools	3·0
	1% other	
24	Morris	0·7[2]
31	Thurmott	0·9[3]
33	Watson	3·0

Notes to Table 17
1. Mid-point of reported range 0–5·7.
2. Includes relaxation/mothercraft 0·4%.
3. Includes only teaching in schools.

teaching; 29 per cent were involved in teaching children in schools, 24 per cent in running parents and mothers clubs, 40 per cent in ante-natal classes, and 6 per cent in post-natal mothercraft sessions. Perkins, who surveyed the health education activities of health visitors in Nottinghamshire in 1977 as part of a larger project concerned specifically with health education in one area health authority (Leverhulme Health Education Project) found that 55 per cent of the 120 respondents were involved in teaching in schools, 77 per cent in ante-natal classes, 34 per cent in sessions with "other learning groups" and 36 per cent undertook "one-off" talks with youth clubs or adult groups. (Perkins 1978).

Studies which are specifically concerned with the health visitor's role in health education include:

Callender, J. (1978)   Health Education in an Obstetric Programme of Care. Eastern Health and Social Services Board, Belfast.

Hall, C. P. (1977)   Health Visitors and Health Education. Unpublished M. Phil. thesis. University of Surrey.

Hobbs, P. (1973)   Aptitude or Environment. London. Rcn.

Perkins, E. R. (1978)   Group Health Education by Health Visitors. University of Nottingham. Leverhulme Trust Health Education Project.

Occasional Paper No. 7 (see also other Occasional Papers in the series concerned with particular types of health education).

CHAPTER 8

Administrative and Clerical Work

In Chapter 3 it was shown that "clerical and administrative duties" accounted for almost as much time as home visiting, and in some studies (e.g. Nos. 7, 22 and 29) it exceeded visiting time. The amount of time spent on clerical work expressed as a proportion of total time was shown in Table 2; the average time per day recorded by nine studies is shown in Table 18.

The range shown in Table 2 is very wide, from 11·4 per cent to 51·7 per cent of total time. This is a reflection not only of actual differences but also of the different category systems used by the various researchers, and for this reason the findings should be interpreted with caution. For example, the high figure of 51·7 per cent reported by Poulton (Study No. 29) includes telephoning (13·7 per cent), meetings

Table 18

Time Spent on Clerical and Administrative Duties: Average Time Per Day
(9 studies)

Study No.	Name of Researcher	Average time per day	
		Hours	Minutes
1	Akester and MacPhail	2	30
2	Allen and King[1]	1	40
9	Clow[2]		55
17	Gilmore et al	1	28
19	Henderson	1	47
21	Loveland	1	14
22	Marris	2	03
29	Poulton	2	40
33	Watson	1	18
	All Studies	1	45

Notes to Table 18
1. Mean of attached and non-attached health visitors.
2. Calculated by division (by 5) of reported weekly average.

(4 per cent), clinical consultation (3·1 per cent) and teaching students (2·2 per cent); when these elements are excluded from the figure for "true" clerical duties it is reduced to 28·7 per cent which is much nearer the mean. The survey itself generates additional clerical work; Allen, King and Abbott (Study No. 3) report that this was 5 per cent of total time, Clow (Study No. 9) reported 4·7 per cent and Marris (Study No. 22) 19 minutes per day.

It is also clear that the averages which are reported by individual studies conceal considerable individual variation. For example, Potton (Study No. 28) reported a range of 12 per cent to 40 per cent; Graham (Study No. 18) a range of 19·5 per cent to 30·1 per cent; Watson (Study No. 33) a range of 16 to 114 minutes per day, and Gilmore et al (Study No. 17) 45 minutes to 142 minutes per day. Watson reported in full the time spent by each of the 21 health visitors in her study and comments:

"Quite a number of health visitors are known to do some office work, particularly writing of records, at home. It is assumed that H.V.3 (16 minutes, and the lower extreme of the range) chooses to allocate the greatest proportion of her work time to home visiting but that this is only possible because she is willing to do most of her writing at home". (Watson, 1977, Page 7).

Marris (Study No. 22) reported that the amount of time spent on clerical work varied with health visitor's work base, borough type, method of transport, and according to whether she was attached to general practice or not. He did not, however, report whether the differences were statistically significant nor did he discuss the possible relationships between these factors.

It is very difficult to interpret all these findings and particularly to explain the wide variation without more detailed information about the content of "clerical work". Few studies report much detail. Watson (Study No. 33) distinguishes between writing (43 minutes per day), reading (10 minutes), telephone (12 minutes), and filing (13 minutes) total 78 minutes per day). Potton (Study No. 28) reports that clerical work included infant visiting cards, clinic records, birth books, appointments, weekly and monthly returns, reports and supplies requisition, but does not specify the allocation of time to each activity. Thorpe (Study No. 30) categorised the clerical tasks undertaken by health visitors as follows:

1. the update of information onto the health visiting record;
2. the provision of information on request, e.g. reports for social services, transfer of records, etc.;
3. the arrangements of appointments and future visits;
4. the compilation of statistics;
5. filing;
6. the distribution of mail.

He reviewed each task and made recommendations, but the report does not include any statistical data or information about the allocation of time.

In the City of Leicester study (Study No. 7) the "excessively high" (41·9 per cent) proportion of time spent performing clerical duties resulted in a secondary survey being conducted to define in detail individual clerical tasks and to determine the time spent performing the tasks. The number of hours per week spent on the various clerical activities is shown in Table 19.

Table 19

Detailed Analysis of Time Spent on Clerical Activities (a) City of Leicester (Study No. 7)

Clerical Activity	Hours per Health Visitor per Week
* Updating records	5·367
* Transferring records	0·646
* Filing records	2·119
Preparing work	1·101
Writing letters	0·896
Sorting post	0·786
Dictating	0·189
Telephone calls	1·204
Time sheets	0·708
* Ministry returns	0·029
Case discussions	1·839
* Clinic appointments	0·245
* Maintaining stores	0·045
Staff meetings	0·706
Completing car log	0·050
TOTAL	15·933

*clerical duties that could be allocated to a clerk/typist.

The researchers concluded that a large proportion of the clerical work undertaken by health visitors could be performed by a clerk/audio typist; the tasks which they suggested could be allocated are marked with an asterisk in the Table. They recommended that additional clerk/audio typists should be established at each of the divisional headquarters, and that the health visitors should be provided with portable tape recorders and the clerks with transcribing equipment. They estimated that if this were done the time spent on clerical duties would be reduced from 41·88 per cent to 18·87 per cent, and the proportion of "effective health visiting time" would be raised by 41 per cent, from 43·54 per cent to 61·38 per cent.

Morris (Study No. 24) also conducted a special survey of clerical work. The distribution of time between the various activities as shown in Table 20.

Table 20

Detailed Analysis of Time Spent on Clerical Activities (b) Morris
(Study No. 24)

	Percentage of clerical time spent on each activity
(a) Maternal and Child Health:	
recording home visits	28·88
planning work	21·69
phone calls	13·14
diary	9·44
taking messages	4·55
new birth forms/cards	3·94
travel expense/leave forms	3·08
writing reports and letters	2·98
transfer of records	2·15
immunisation records	1·16
sending out appointments	1·25
hospital liason referrals	0·84
monthly N.A.I. forms	0·36
special follow-up forms	0·30
weekly immigration return	0·18
T.B. notifications	0·01
other activities	2·73
(b) School Health:	
preparation for health education	0·73
recording vision tests	0·66
phone calls	0·54
parental permission forms	0·32
immunisation forms	0·32
recording home visits	0·21
writing hygiene letters	0·09
Total maternal and child health clerical work	97·13
Total school health clerical work	2·87
TOTAL CLERICAL WORK	100·00

Source: Morris (1970) (Study No. 2).

Poulton (Study No. 29) provides some further detail on the question of meetings. She reported that meetings occurred on 20 per cent of the recorded days, and lasted on average one hour 20 minutes each. Twenty-eight per cent (whether the percentages are percentages of the total numbers of meetings or of the time spent on meetings is not clear) were full staff meetings, 50 per cent were "ad hoc/nursing officer" meetings, 7 per cent were "clinical discussion" (presumably this is in addition to the 3·1 per cent of total time separately recorded as "clinical consultation"),

5 per cent were with social workers, 5 per cent were general practitioners, and 5 per cent inservice training.

Several researchers comment on the necessity for clerical help for health visitors, and Allen, King and Abbott (Study No. 3) reported that 55 per cent of health visitors in their study had some clerical help available, and 28 per cent had dictating facilities, but the effect of this upon the amount of time spent by the health visitors on their clerical work is not known.

Discussion

Several researchers have commented adversely on the "high" proportion of time spent by health visitors on clerical work and have used their findings to argue the need for the provision of clerical help. Gallaher *et al* (Study No. 13) reported that in their establishment of "target times" the amount of time allocated for clerical work was reduced by half, but they do not specify what measures were used to achieve this aim.

It must be appreciated, however, that the interpretation of the recorded proportions as "high" is a value judgement. On the one hand it can be argued that reduction in the time spent on clerical work would enable more time to be spent on more highly valued activities such as home visiting. There is no guarantee that this would happen in practice, and although Gallaher *et al* (Study No. 13) showed that following the establishment of performance targets this did happen, Marris (Study No. 22) found that the proportion of time devoted to clerical work was inversely related not with home visiting time but with travelling time. On the other hand it could be argued that time on clerical work is closely related to "time at base" which is necessary for the acceptance of referrals and the exercise of the health visitor's liason role (Chapter 10). It could also be argued that "clerical activities" is a residual category which covers "intervals between client contacts" (Marris specifically reports that this is included in his category of general administration) which provides the respite or recovery periods necessary for adequate performance during the next period of client contact. These ideas are at present purely speculative. The truth is that we do not know what is the "right" level of clerical activity, and much more information is necessary for such judgements to be soundly based.

More information is necessary to determine which, if any, of the clerical tasks undertaken by health visitors could be delegated to other people. Morris (Study No. 24) reported that the three major components of clerical activity were recording home visits (28·9 per cent plus a further 0·2 per cent on school health home visits), planning work (21·7 per cent plus 0·7 per cent on preparation for health education), and telephone calls (13·1 per cent plus 0·5 per cent on school health phone calls). It is arguable whether these activities, which together constitute two thirds (65·1 per cent) of all clerical activities recorded by Morris, could be delegated to other people. Morris comments:

"Nearly 29 per cent of clerical time is taken up by recording home visits. This can only be done by the relevant health visitor and recent events have highlighted the importance of accurate record keeping. One way to economise in this time would be the use of Grundig Notebooks (pocket dictation machines) which, if acceptable to the health visitors, would involve a considerable amount of secretarial time . . . Reports and letters (3 per cent of clerical time) must be *written* by health visitors, but they still need to be typed".

Dictating facilities are known to be used by health visitors in some areas; Allen, King and Abbott (Study No. 3) reported that 28 per cent of the health visitors in their study already had such facilities in 1969. Bailey and Rawlinson (1969) have discussed the use of dictaphones in health visiting. They found that where health visitors used dictaphones, four main benefits accrued:

1. more concise and factual information was produced;
2. the margin of error was reduced by immediate recording;
3. the typed information, once recorded, was legible at all times to everyone;
4. the time saved enabled a greater volume of work to be done which required the specialised training of the health visitor, in particular home visiting.

A similar investigation was undertaken by the St Thomas' Health District in 1978.

The use of dictating machines might prove to be valuable not only for the reduction of the amount of time spent on clerical work but also to improve the accuracy, completeness, and therefore usefulness of the records themselves. The inadequacy of health visiting records was noted in Chapter 4 of this review.

The allocation of a large proportion of total time to clerical work has other implications also, as Henderson (Study No. 19) has pointed out:

"If it is really essential that health visitors spend so much of their time undertaking administrative duties, then greater emphasis must be placed on preparing them for this aspect of their work during their courses". (Henderson, 1977, Page 29).

The lack of information about clerical work available from the research so far may reflect the low value which health visitors themselves place upon this aspect of their work. Whatever the value accorded to it, and whether the proportion is judged to be "too high" or not, further research into this area of health visiting activity is clearly needed. It is also worthy of note that this aspect of the health visitor's work, unlike most other aspects, is susceptible to orthodox and well-validated work study techniques.

CHAPTER 9

Travel

The proportion of time spent by health visitors on travelling was shown in Table 2 to range from 9 per cent (Study No. 16) to 19 per cent (Study No. 37) with a mean of 13·5 per cent. Little further detail is reported in the studies included in this review, although a specific study of nurses' travel has recently been undertaken by the D.H.S.S.

The three variables most obviously related to travelling time are whether the study was conducted in a rural or an urban area, the means of transport used, and whether the health visitor works in attachment to general practice or within a specified geographical area. The effect of attachment on travelling time is discussed in Chapter 13.

It is difficult to attribute differences in travelling time reported in the various studies solely to differences in the location of the study because the studies themselves differ so widely. Moreover geography obviously affects the choice of means of transport. Akester and MacPhail (Study No. 1) reported of their study in Leeds:

"The daily summaries showed that health visitors who used cars spent as much time travelling as those who used public transport. The reason for this apparent paradox is that health visitors who used cars work in the scattered areas on the city outskirts, or undertake special duties such as tuberculosis or venereal disease visiting. It can be said, however, that health visitors who have cars travelled much greater distances than their colleagues who used public transport, in slightly less time". (Akester and MacPhail, 1961, Page 18).

Marris (Study No. 22) similarly reports of his study in London:

"Cars were much more frequently used as a means of transport in the outer boroughs—three quarters used them there—than in the central boroughs were three quarters of health visitors went on foot. Health visitors in the middle boroughs lay roughly between these two extremes. Bearing in mind, then, this marked difference in the means of travel in different types of borough it is very revealing that travel time did not differ according to type of borough. On the other hand, time did differ very substantially for those few health visitors who used public transport. The 6 per cent of health visitors going mainly by public transport spent 15 per cent of their time in travelling compared with about 10 per cent spent by health visitors going other ways—by car, bicycle or on foot—and the average duration of a journey for those travelling by public transport was nearly double that for those travelling by car or by bicycle . . . The implication is that by one means or another most health visitors in each type of borough found the method that minimised travel time in their locality". (Marris, 1971, Page 32).

Only one study (No. 2) reported mileage. Allen, King (No. 2) reported a daily mileage ranging from 11·2 miles per day to 14·5 miles per day in two rather similar urban areas (St. Albans and Hemel Hempstead). Clearly the daily mileage in a rural area such as Central Wales would be much greater. Potton (Study No. 28) reported that the average time spent on travel showed little variation between the three Districts studied (16·1 per cent, 15·2 per cent, 16·8 per cent) although the geographical areas varied considerably in size and content (256 square miles, 288 square miles, 425 square miles); he calculated the average travel time for each visit made as 12·5 minutes. He noted that there were wide variations between individual staff, but suggested that the spread of the practice population rather than bad organisation of daily routine was the main contributory factor. Poulton (Study No. 29), in an inner city area, found a similar journey time of 12 minutes per visit, and noted that there was no significant difference in the percentage of time spent on travel between those who travelled by car, bus or on foot; like Potton she noted wide individual variation.

CHAPTER 10

The Health Visitor as Liaison Agent: Contact with Other Agencies

Gilmore *et al* (Study No. 17) found that over 60 per cent of the general practitioners and health visitors in the 39 teams which they surveyed considered that health visitors should act as sources of information within their teams on the range of social services available, and in all the teams the health visitors were ranked as being most likely to be primarily allocated this sphere of responsibility. They also reported that while less than a third of general practitioners and approximately two thirds of the district nurses in the 39 teams expressed interest in work involving liason with other agencies, 93 per cent of the health visitors declared themselves to be "interested" or "very interested". Clark (Study No. 8) showed that health visitors were, in fact, in frequent contact with a wide range of agencies; 85 per cent of the health visitors in her sample had been in contact with ten or more agencies during the previous month and almost half (48 per cent) had been in contact with ten or more agencies during the previous week.

Table 21 shows that health visitors appear to spend approximately one tenth of their working time on collaboration and consultation of this kind. The studies are listed in the Table in chronological order, and this

Table 21

Time Spent on Consultation with Other Agencies (7 studies)

Study No.	Name of Researcher	Date of Study	Percentage of time spent on consultation
3	Allen, King and Abbott	1969	3·9
22	Marris	1969	10·3
5	Atkinson	1970	6·2
19	Henderson	1975	10·0
33	Watson	1975	8·9
29	Poulton	1976	11·0
28	Potton	1977–78	12·9

arrangement does appear to show a considerable change over time. Caution is, however, needed in interpreting the figures because the category systems are not necessarily directly comparable; for example, some studies record "telephone time" separately, others include it in "clerical/administrative time", others include it in "consultation time".

Gilmore *et al* (Study No. 17) reported that in all of their 39 teams the telephone was the most common method of communication with outside agencies. Clark (Study No. 8) reported that 48 per cent of contacts with four selected agencies (Childrens' Department, Welfare Department, hospital social workers, and voluntary organisations) were made by telephone, 13·3 per cent were written, and 32·9 per cent were face-to-face. Watson (Study No. 33) recorded a higher proportion of face-to-face contact (46·6 per cent) probably because her table included contacts between the health visitor and other members of the primary care team while Clark's figures refer specifically to selected external agencies.

Allen, King and Abbott (Study No. 3) and Poulton (Study No. 29) specify the division of consultation time between the various agencies. Allen, King and Abbott reported that approximately 43 per cent of this time was spent in consultation with G.P.'s, 38 per cent in consultation with social workers, and 18 per cent in consultation with senior nurse managers. Poulton reported that 25 per cent was spent on case conferences, 24 per cent with the general practitioner, 20 per cent with volunteers (including neighbours), 1 per cent with social workers (other than at case conferences) and 20 per cent with others. Gilmore *et al* (Study No. 17) reported that in the three centres in their study the highest number of contacts with external agencies was with social work departments. The figures are difficult to interpret because different studies use different bases for their calculation (e.g. some include and others exclude contacts within the primary care team) and there is not always a clear differentiation made between consultation and referral.

Both Watson and Clark reported that the health visitor was usually the initiator of the communication. In Watson's study 343 contacts were made by health visitors compared with 153 received; Clark reported that the health visitor initiated 72 per cent of the contacts with the Childrens' Department, 78 per cent of the contacts with the Welfare Department, 83 per cent of the contacts with voluntary organisations but only 28 per cent of the contacts with hospital social workers.

Although the distinction between consultation and referral is not always clear, the findings of eight studies which provide information about referrals or contacts made subsequent to client contact are listed in Table 22. Allen and King (Study No. 2) reported that their health visitors made on average 3·25 referrals per month to social workers and that this rate was higher than the rate of referrals to the general practitioner. Four studies (Nos. 3, 25, 32 and 33) report the percentage of visits which were followed by referral to another agency: Naidoo (Study No. 25) reported 41·9 per cent, Walworth-Bell (Study No. 32) 34 per cent, and Watson

Table 22

Contacts Made by Health Visitors Subsequent to Client Consultation (8 studies)

Study No.	Name of Researcher	G.P.	Other Health Services or Health Workers	Social Workers/ Social Services	Other
23	Ministry of Health	22	23	47	13
1	Akester and MacPhail[1]	14·6	66·6	14·6	4·2
16	Gilmore	63·1	20·4	6·1	10·6
3	Allen, King and Abbott	2·4	Not Specified	2·7	Not Specified
8	Clark[2]	21·3	30·1	26·0	22·6
17	Gilmore et al[3]	Not Specified	22·5	50·8	26·7
33	Watson	29·3	15·2	8·1	47·4
32	Walworth-Bell	32·2	25·6	17·9	24·2

Notes to Table 22
1. Based on Akester and MacPhail Table XII—48 contacts made after 39 out of the 93 visits to babies under 1 month.
2. Total number of contacts was 362.
3. 386 contacts made following 1991 visits in three centres; excludes contacts with other members of the primary health care team.

63

(Study No. 33) 25 per cent; Allen, King and Abbott (Study No. 3) reported that 15 per cent of adults and 2·7 per cent of children visited were referred.

Discussion

Henderson (Study No. 19) commented that, at 10 per cent of the total, the time spent on this activity "seemed high" and speculated on the reasons as follows:

> "One wonders if it is associated with the management structure now existing in the nursing profession. Unfortunately there are no possible comparisons between the pre- and post- Mayston situation. There is also the possibility of increased consultation in primary health care teams, to the ultimate benefit of clients. A third possibility is the increase in the number of situations where there is some legal involvement for the health visitor which requires consultation with senior members of staff. These suggestions are purely conjecural but might be worth further consideration". (Henderson, 1978, Page 32).

It is, unfortunately, quite impossible to tease out of the available data the separate strands of communication and consultation with colleagues which Henderson points out. It is likely, however, that administrative policies such as the development of the concepts of multidisciplinary teamwork and the primary health care team, the machinery established for the prevention and management of non-accidental injury to children, and changes in the management structure of the community nursing services must exert a considerable influence, and these factors alone might explain the apparent increase during the past decade in the proportion of their time which health visitors spent on this activity.

CHAPTER 11

The Content of Health Visiting

The question "What do health visitors do?" is usually answered in terms of the time allocated to various activities or in terms of the clientele visited. These two responses to the question are described in Chapters 3 and 4. Such answers are, however, very incomplete, for each begs further questions such as "What are health visitors actually doing when they are in contact with child clients and how does this differ from what they are doing when they are in contact with elderly clients?".

These questions are much more difficult to answer because the data required demand observational methods. This problem was discussed in Chapter 2 of this review. Only one observational study of the work of the health visitor has so far been undertaken (Study No. 30) but its findings should for that reason be carefully noted even though its sample was small, self-selected, and limited to one Scottish town.

Basing her methods on traditional work-study techniques, Watson writes:

"The first step in a time study is to prepare a comprehensive activity classification. Each of these activities must have a start and finish sufficiently sharp to be accurately timed; the sequence and duration of activities can thus be noted and measured. . . Visits do not, of course, consist merely of a sequence of activities. Their emphasis is on creating a communicating relationship through which needs can be assessed and met and this leads to a consideration of the second major focus of interest—that of topic. The topics raised by client and health visitor were noted and timed in a similar way to the activities." (Watson, 1977, Page 1–2).

This approach to the analysis of health visiting activity was also used by Clark (Study No. 8), who did not, however, use observational methods. Clark wrote:

"Health appraisal, health teaching, providing emotional support, and social counselling—the expressed aims of the home visit—can be successfully accomplished only through communication with the client. The verbal behaviour of health visitors and their clients in face to face contact in the home visit is the major, though not the only, component in such communication. Verbal behaviour may be classified according to the subject matter discussed, the time devoted to each item, the relative contribution of participants, the mechanisms of communication (questioning, advising, etc.), the expressions of affect (especially anxiety or hostility), forms of reassurance, instances of laughter and of silence." (Clark, 1973, Page 55).

Clark reports that the idea of measuring the content of the home visit in terms of the topics discussed and the communication techniques used was suggested by Johnson and Hardin's study of the work of American public Health Nurses (Johnson and Hardin, 1962). The approach is, in fact, incorporated into the title of their published report "*Content and Dynamics* of Home Visits of Public Health Nurses". The idea and methodology developed by Clark was subsequently copied by Marris (Study No. 22), but with some modifications of categories and with a different method of presenting the data so that the two studies are not directly comparable. Clark's schema, with some minor modifications, was also used by Naidoo (Study No. 25), but the way in which Naidoo's data are presented (percentages without raw scores) prevents detailed comparison with either study.

Topics Discussed by Health Visitors

Table 23 shows the incidence of topics recorded in home visits of various kinds. Clark presents the subject matter of the home visit by showing how often particular topics occurred in the 2,057 home visits recorded, and in various subgroups within the total sample; this frequency expressed as a percentage of the total number of visits within the group is referred to as the "topic incidence". This method of presentation permits comparisons between visits of various kinds, e.g. to different kinds of households, visits initiated by the general practitioner, or visits made by different kinds of health visitors. Detailed comparisons of this kind are included in Clark (1973), but are beyond the scope of this review.

This method of presentation takes no account of the time spent in discussion of the various topics nor, therefore, of the relative importance of each topic within the discussion. Marris (Study No. 22) incorporated time in his study, and his results are presented (Table 24) both in terms of "frequency" and in terms of the time spent on each topic.

However, although his text (Page 34) refers to frequency, that is, the $(\frac{\text{number of occurrences}}{\text{number of visits}})$; the Table presents the data as a proportion of all topics recorded; that is, the $(\frac{\text{number of occurrences of individual topic}}{\text{total number of topics recorded}})$ and the given percentage figure may, therefore, be distorted by under- or over-recording of the total. For example, if immunisation is discussed nine times in 100 visits, whatever else is discussed the topic incidence for "immunisation" is 9 per cent. If 600 topics are recorded during the 100 visits, Marris' method of analysis would yield a figure of 1·5 per cent. If, however, only 300 topics are recorded during the 100 visits (perhaps because the category system was inadequate or because of selectivity of

Table 23

Topics Discussed in Home Visits (Clark 1976)

Incidence of topics recorded in home visits to different types of household (number of occurrences recorded expressed as percentage of number of visits recorded in each group)

Topic	Households containing young child (1,452 visits)	containing elderly (370 visits)	Other households (225 visits)	All households (2,057* visits)
1. Diet—child under 1 year	51·9	0·5	0	36·8
2. Diet—child 1–4 years	21·1	0·3	0·4	15·1
3. Development—physical	50·3	0·5	2·2	35·9
4. Development—mental and emotional	36·0	0·3	3·1	25·8
5. Emotional/behaviour problem (under 5 years)	15·8	0·3	1·3	11·4
6. Immunisation	43·7	0	1·3	31·1
7. Screening procedure	23·4	0·3	0·4	16·7
8. Minor ailments (under 5 years)	13·4	0	0·9	9·6
9. Specific illness (under 5 years)	12·2	0·3	1·3	8·8
10. Daily minding/day nursery	3·9	0	1·3	2·9
11. Playgroup/nursery school	16·1	0·5	0·9	11·5
12. Fostering/adoption	3·7	0·3	2·2	2·9
13. Child cruelty/neglect	1·5	0	1·3	1·2
14. Preparation for school	8·0	0	2·2	5·9
15. Other topic (child under 5 years)	5·5	0·3	0·4	4·0
16. General health	31·5	38·1	40·9	33·6
17. General hygiene	3·9	7·0	3·1	4·5
18. Diet (over 5 years)	6·7	39·2	18·7	13·8
19. Specific illness (over 5 years)	7·1	50·3	35·1	17·9
21. Behaviour problems—child over 5 years	6·9	0·5	12·0	6·3
22. Behaviour problem—adolescent	1·6	0·3	8·4	2·1
23. Behaviour problem—adult	4·1	5·4	5·3	4·5
24. Mental illness—frank	3·0	2·2	12·4	3·8
25. Mental illness—latent	3·8	3·8	5·8	4·0
26. Mental subnormality	2·4	0·3	4·9	2·3
27. School	9·4	1·1	19·6	9·0
28. Expectant mother—physical care	4·8	0·3	4·4	3·9
29. Expectant mother—mental care	3·6	0·3	4·0	3·0
30. Post-natal mother—physical care	23·7	0·5	1·3	17·0
31. Post-natal mother—mental care	16·2	1·1	0·9	11·8

*In ten schedules the type of household was not recorded.

67

Table 23 (continued)

Incidence of topics recorded in home visits to different types of household (number of occurrences recorded expressed as percentage of number of visits recorded in each group)

Topic	Households containing young child (1,452 visits)	containing elderly (370 visits)	Other households (225 visits)	All households (2,057* visits)
32. Nursing care	1·7	26·2	12·0	7·2
33. Adjustment to illness/handicap	3·1	35·1	22·2	11·0
34. Adjustment to recent marriage	0·7	0	2·2	0·8
35. Marital disharmony	8·4	1·9	9·3	7·3
36. Family planning	14·9	0	3·6	10·9
37. Menopause	0·3	0·5	3·1	0·7
38. Adjustment to/preparation for retirement	0	5·4	3·1	1·3
39. Bereavement	1·3	7·8	3·6	2·8
40. Other (health) topic	3·7	9·5	6·7	5·0
41. Employment	11·8	1·9	21·5	11·2
42. Housing	18·9	19·2	20·4	19·2
43. Financial inadequacy	7·8	8·6	14·7	8·7
44. Financial management	3·4	1·6	6·2	3·5
45. Social Security benefits	4·2	15·9	13·3	7·3
46. Legal problem	4·5	3·0	6·2	4·4
47. Household management	7·5	14·3	13·3	9·4
48. Home help	5·7	54·9	30·2	17·3
49. Home safety	8·2	13·2	5·8	8·8
50. Relationship building†	—	—	—	—
51. Other	6·6	28·1	14·7	11·4

*In ten schedules the type of household was not recorded.
†This topic was excluded from all analyses.

recording), the same raw data subjected to Marris' method of analysis would produce the different figure of 3 per cent. For this reason Marris' data on the "frequency" of the various topics are very difficult to interpret.

Moreover, even assuming the validity of the raw scores, the analysis of the time component reduces the validity of the data as presented. Marris reports:

"The time taken for the act of service was also recorded, and this was divided up between the topics on the assumption that during that particular act of service each topic took the same length of time.... The length of time allocated to each topic is, therefore, the number of minutes for the act of service divided by the number of topics covered." (Marris, 1971, Page 34).

Table 24

Topics Recorded by Health Visitors and Time Spent on Each Topic
(Marris 1971)

Topic	Number of topics	Time spent on topics
Total	88,906 topics 100%	406,080 minutes 100%
	%	%
Child management		
Infant management and diet and minor health problems	14·3	16·0
Toddler management and diet and minor health problems	8·0	7·9
Child-minding or nursery school or play group	4·1	4·8
Home safety	1·5	1·6
School progress	1·3	1·4
Fostering or adoption	0·6	0·8
Child cruelty or neglect	0·6	0·9
Screening		
Other screening test carried out or discussed	8·1	4·5
School medical inspection (health screening)	6·6	3·6
Phenylketonuria test carried out	1·6	1·3
Health		
Other health poroblems—children	5·4	4·6
Other health problems—adults	3·3	4·5
Clinic	2·5	2·4
Nursing care or hospital aftercare	1·6	1·9
Communicable disease (not V.D.)	1·2	0·9
Provision of aids	0·6	0·9
Immunisation		
Immunisation or vaccination discussed	9·0	7·2
Immunisation or vaccination carried out	2·1	1·5
Social services		
Financial, legal, employment, housing problems	3·7	5·0
Dealings with other official bodies	2·1	2·5
Problems of being unsupported or needing social services	2·0	2·5
Problems of being old	0·9	1·5
Problems of being an immigrant	0·9	0·9
Mental health		
Emotional or mental problems (not subnormality)	3·9	4·9
Enuretic problems	0·9	0·9
Adjustment to recent handicap or chronic illness	0·6	0·8
Adjustment to recent bereavement	0·3	0·5
Mental subnormality	0·4	0·6

Table 24 (continued)

	Number of topics	Time spent on topics
Total	**88,906 topics 100%**	**406,080 minutes 100%**
Topic	%	%
Marital problems		
Family planning (not abortion)	2·6	2·9
Marriage guidance	0·7	1·1
Miscarriage, infertility, gynaecology, etc.	0·7	0·8
Request for advice on abortion	0·2	0·3
Advice on actual or suspected V.D.	0·1	0·1
First contact		
First involvement with person and introductory discussion	4·1	4·5
Diet		
Adult's diet or vitamins	2·4	2·5
School child's diet or vitamins	0·8	0·8
Drink and drugs		
Alcoholism	0·1	0·2
Drug addiction	0·1	0·2

Source: Marris (1971) Table 16 page 35.

The assumption of equal time between topics cannot be supported and the figures are, therefore, misleading.

The data on the subject matter discussed in home visits which is most valid and reliable is probably that provided by Watson (Study No. 33). Watson's category system is less detailed than that of Clark and Marris, but its validity is probably greater because it was developed from the two hundred different topics recorded by means of direct observation during pilot studies. The category system developed by Watson was as follows:

1. reproduction
2. infancy
3. childhood
4. problems associated with ageing and handicap
5. "health"
6. "illness"
7. emotional factors and behavioural problems
8. immunisation
9. accident prevention
10. income/finance/occupation
11. housing/home situation

12. services and service providers
13. anything else.

Watson's findings are shown in Table 25. In addition to the data shown in the Tables, other researchers have reported as follows:

1. Ambler *et al* (Study No. 4) found that topics relating to health or illness were discussed in 95 per cent of visits. An illness or its treatment was discussed on 47 per cent of visits recorded in one town, 38 per cent of visits in the second town and 34 per cent in the third town. The comparable figures for visits where children under five were discussed were 38 per cent, 32 per cent and 30 per cent.

2. Allen, King and Abbott (Study No. 3) found that advice on topics of health and/or illness was given in 66 per cent of visits to families with social problems, and in 90 per cent where the family also contained a child.

3. Gilmore *et al* (Study No. 17) report that "health counselling" occurred in 91 per cent of the visits at Centre A, 95 per cent of those at Centre B, and 79 per cent of those at Centre C; "advise on social problems" occurred in 9 per cent of the visits at Centre A, 11 per cent at Centre B, and 25 per cent at Centre C.

4. Naidoo (Study No. 25), using the visit schedule developed by Clark (Study No. 8), found that "physical health topics" were discussed in 86·9 per cent of visits, "emotional health topics" in 50·3 per cent of visits, and "social care topics" in 66·4 per cent of visits. The comparable findings reported by Clark are that "emotional health topics" were recorded in 59·1 per cent of visits, and "social care topics" in 65·8 per cent of visits; the proportion of visits in which

Table 25

Topics Discussed in Home Visits (Watson 1977)

Topic group	Percentage of visits which this topic group was main topic group
Infancy (Feeding, development, screening)	26[1]
Child care (speech development, etc.)	17[1]
Services and services providers	17
Illness (symptoms, diagnosis, treatment, etc.)	15
Psycho/social (emotional and behavioural)	12
Problems, income and finance	13
TOTAL	100%

Notes to Table 25
1. "If topic groups 2 and 3 are totalled, these are the main topics of discussion in 43% of all visits, and in 67% of visits to families with children under school age".

71

"physical health topics" were discussed is not recorded. The similarity between the two sets of figures obtained by the same recording instrument and analysed by the same category system increases the probability of validity.

Techniques and Action

Analysis of what Johnson and Hardin (1962) called the "dynamics" of health visiting activity is probably the most difficult aspect of the health visitor's work to describe or analyse, and very few researchers have attempted the task.

Activities were recorded and categorised at a relatively simple level in Study Nos. 1, 13, 17, and 29, but the category systems used are inadequate, and because they differ from one another the findings cannot be compared. Wiseman (Study No. 36) asked her respondents to specify their "function" (categorised under 14 headings) in each visit recorded, but this concept is probably more similar to that of "purpose" (see Chapter 5) than that of "technique".

Clark (1973) was particularly interested in describing the "dynamics" in terms which could be related to the "didactic and authoritarian approach" which was one component of the stereotype of the health visitor. Johnson and Hardin (1962) had developed a series of indices for measuring various dimensions of "verbal involvement", including a "dominance dimension" and a "teaching or health counselling dimension" and Clark adapted these to a simpler form which could be self-recorded. The variables used were the initiation of the subject matter (whether the topic was raised by the health visitor or by the client) and three "Levels of verbal involvement" defined as follows

Level 1   Listening and reassurance only
Level 2   Discussion plus factual information
Level 3   Discussion plus positive advice or teaching.

Clark's findings are reported in detail and carefully discussed in her book and are beyond the scope of this review. In summary, however, she found that health visitors initiated just over half (57·2 per cent) of all the topics recorded, and that 39·9 per cent of topics were dealt with by listening and reassurance only, 36·2 per cent by discussion and factual information, and 19·0 per cent by advice or teaching. The relative proportions varied greatly, however, with individual topics, when the topics were grouped into "physical health", "mental health" and "social care" topics, and in different kinds of visits. Naidoo (Study No. 24) used the same method of recording but presented the results differently and the findings cannot, therefore, be compared.

Developing the same idea, Marris (Study No. 22) developed a more detailed category system of 15 "techniques" grouped under the three main headings "communication", "application" and "co-ordination". He reported that 54·5 per cent of the techniques recorded were in the "communication" group, 34·8 per cent in the "application" group and 10·7 per cent in the "co-ordination" group.

Watson (Study No. 33) developed an activity classification, based on observations made during pilot studies, using ten categories as follows: questioning (and listening to answers); listening; information; advice; reassurance; comment; service; examination; social chat; talking to children.

Unfortunately, Watson's findings are reported only in broad outline:

"Listening was the main activity of the health visitor in 52 per cent of the visits. In 22 per cent of visits questioning was the main activity, these visits were mainly to families with a young baby. (In visits to adults and to the over 80's, it was particularly likely that listening was the main activity.) In 13 per cent of visits social chat was the main activity—there was an even spread through all client age groups. It must be pointed out, however, that this may be a valuable means of establishing and maintaining a relationship in addition to assisting in the assessment of socio-psychological well-being. The visits in which information giving was the main activity (6 per cent) were mainly to primigravidae and to families with one child only." (Watson, 1977, Pages 9–10).

Action Subsequent to the Home Visit

The health visitor's work in relation to a consultation with a client, whether at a home visit, in a child health clinic or elsewhere, does not end with the consultation. Study Nos. 1, 3, 8, 22, 23, 25, 32 and 33 give some information about subsequent action. The action reported is usually "consultation", "follow-up", or "refer", but the three categories overlap and are differently grouped in the various studies so that comparison between studies is not possible. However, the proportion of visits following which no subsequent action (other than recording the visit) was taken was reported by five studies as follows:

Akester and MacPahil (Study No.1)	47·5%
Clark (Study No. 8)	36·3%
Jameson Report (Study No. 23)	72·0%.
Naidoo (Study No. 25)	13·0%
Watson (Study No. 33)	76·0%

Discussion

To describe and analyse the content of the health visitor's work in greater detail than the broad categories of activity described in Chapter 3 of this review is an extremely difficult task. The task is probably not susceptible to survey methods of investigation. Even if observational methods are used—and only one small scale study, that of Watson, has so far attempted to use observational methods—the development of an adequate category system is necessary to enable data to be presented in a way which is meaningful to the average reader.

All the data presented here, however, in spite of the methodological difficulties, point to the general conclusion that the range of work is very wide and is not easily encompassed in traditional or current role prescriptions or by what Clark (1973) has described as the "stereotype" of health visiting.

Moreover, there is evidence, discernible in several of the individual studies, that the work content varies considerably between *individual health visitors.* Clark (1973), for example, showed that there were major differences in the content and organisation of visits recorded by health visitors of different ages and different types of training; she argued the existence of a "new breed" health visitor. Marris found similar differences between work recorded in inner, central and outer boroughs, and although he argued that these differences were due to geography, it could be argued that at least some of the variation was due to differences in the health visitors which, in fact, were highly correlated with the geographical differences (e.g. the older, more experienced health visitors were mainly in the outer boroughs). The width of the ranges reported by Watson (Study No. 33) and Graham (Study No. 18) further confirms this view. Some of the variation may be explained by geographical differences as suggested by Marris, and by organisational differences such as attachment to general practice (discussed in Chapter 13 of this review), but quite clearly the clinical independence which is an essential feature of health visiting practice must play a large part in determining work content. Variations due to this source, while crucial to the understanding and evaluation of health visiting practice, are not detectable in large scale survey methods of investigation.

CHAPTER 12

Does Attachment Make a Difference?

Eleven of the 37 studies included in this review were specifically concerned with the effect of attachment on the work of the health visitor. These were studies Nos. 2, 4, 5, 9, 10, 12, 18, 25, 29, 32 and 37. Two of these, however, (Nos. 12 and 37) reported on the work of attached health visitors without any comparisons with non-attached health visitors. Four further studies (Nos. 8, 19, 22 and 33) included comparative data which may contribute to such assessment. This chapter is, therefore, based on the data reported by 13 studies, only four of which were available to Hawthorn in her review (Hawthorn 1971).

A number of studies have investigated the opinions of doctors and nurses about attachment, and the extent of attachment schemes. Most of these were published before 1970 and were included in Hawthorn's review. This review is limited to analysis of the health visitor's work; in the studies which included both opinions about attachment and information about the health visitor's work (e.g. Nos. 4, 29 and 32) only the information about the health visitor's work is included here.

It has proved impossible to collate the findings of these 13 studies in such a way as to provide comparative data in tabular form as was done, for example, in Chapters 3 and 4. The studies themselves are too diverse and the samples are small. For this reason each study is briefly described (for further summaries see Appendix B) and the findings are then brought together under general headings as follows:

    (a) allocation of time to various activities
    (b) clientele
    (c) travel
    (d) consultation and communication with G.P.s
    (e) referrals
    (f) content/orientation of work

The studies are first considered in chronological order:

1. Study No. 18—Graham (data: 1965)

Graham analysed the work of two recently attached health visitors and six non-attached health visitors in Worthing "comparing non-attached health visitors' work with that of attached health visitors, before embarking on further attachments". His account is very brief and the data are very imprecise (ranges only given), but he reported the time spent on various activities and the "pattern of visiting", and concluded that both groups of health visitors spent too much time on clerical duties and that visiting the elderly seemed to be becoming an increasingly important aspect of the health visitor's work.

2. Study No. 2—Allen and King (data: 1965–66)

Allen and King studied the work of health visitors in two areas within the same county in two surveys separated by an interval of one year. At the time of the first survey the health visitors in one area were attached, in the other area not attached; by the time of the second survey both groups of health visitors were attached. The sample size was very small: ten health visitors in each area for the first survey, 13 and 17 for the second survey. The researchers reported that for this reason "the findings were not subjected to statistical analysis"; the data are presented for each of the four sub-groups separately. The findings include information on the allocation of time to various activities, clientele, travelling, consultation, and referral. The authors conclude:

"The survey has shown that the range and amount of work carried out by health visitors increased following attachment to general practitioners, that more time has been spent in consultation with G.P.s and that more referrals took place between H.V. and G.P. The number of referrals made by health visitors to social workers also increased . . . Travelling time and mileage were not found to increase significantly with the attachment schemes. The small scale of the study has made statistical analysis and deduction of firm conclusions difficult. The need for a large scale study is evident". (Allen and King, 1968, Page 179).

3. Study No. 9—Clow (data: 1966)

Clow studied the work of 48 health visitors (24 attached, 24 non-attached) from six divisions in the West Riding of Yorkshire "to assess whether there had been any reorientation in the deployment of the health visitor as a result of attachment". He compared the time spent by the two groups on various activities, the clientele of the health visitor's home visits, travel and consultation and referral patterns. He concluded:

"In this survey the main points of difference would appear to be that the attached health visitor does an increased amount of clinic work (both at L.H.A. clinics and in the general practitioner's surgery) but less visiting. There is a reduction in the under-five visiting but a small increase in visits to the over 65's, if home help visiting is excluded. The attached nurse spends more time in consulting her various professional and lay colleagues; her travelling time was slightly less but her mileage greater. Clerical work, schools and health education were the same in both groups. In short such differences as are apparent are only marginal". (Clow, 1968, Page 164).

4. Study No. 5—Atkinson 1 (data: 1970)

Four years later, Atkinson surveyed the work of health visitors in the same area "to review the overall volume of work, detect any new trends arising from working in general practice situations to see what work could be delegated by health visitors to assistants". This time a much larger sample was used (264 health visitors) although details of how it was drawn were not specified. Surprisingly, in view of the stated aim of the survey, no comparative data is reported. Atkinson remarks:

"It will be noted that figures given relate to the whole country and are not separately given for staff attachment and unattached to general practices. The differences were surprisingly small . . . The survey showed no demonstrably new trends arising from attachment to general practice. Increased geriatric visiting has taken place wherever good relationships exist between general practitioners and local authority staff and not only where full attachment arrangements are in force. Greater understanding can well develop from using the same building, and the benefits originally associated with full attachment may then develop to some degree".

5. Study No. 4—Ambler et al (data: 1967)

Ambler *et al* compared the work of 22 health visitors in a county borough in which all the health visitors were attached (Town A) with the work of health visitors in two other county boroughs of similar size and social structure. In both of these towns the health visitors worked in traditional geographical districts, but in one of them (Town D1) five of the 16 health visitors were working in "liason" schemes. The researchers discussed the health visitors' allocation of time to various activities, their clientele, and communication patterns with general practitioners and other agencies. They concluded:

"While it has been possible to show that the patterns of work were different, it is much more difficult to demonstrate that any differences have been caused by attachment. The different staffing levels of the three towns and the organisation and policies of the L.H.A.'s are among the factors which affect the work being done". (Ambler *et al*, 1968, Page 298).

6. Study No. 10—Dawtrey (data: 1975)

Dawtrey analysed a one in five sample of the case records of two health visitors (one attached, one non-attached) in one health centre "with particular emphasis on the two contrasting ways of organising her work". Statistically significant differences were found in the "origin of last contact" (i.e. type of case) and in the "reason for last contact", but the data were too inadequate for any conclusions to be drawn.

7. Study No. 29—Poulton (data: 1975)

Poulton studied the work of 10 attached and 44 "aligned" health visitors "to determine the operation and effectiveness of the existing community nursing services relating to different organisational structures in the Wandsworth and East Merton Teaching District". This study tested all the differences reported for statistical significance, although the level of probability chosen to establish significance was higher than is usually used (p = ·05). Poulton concluded:

> "The aligned health visitor seems to spend slightly more time on clinical activities than her attached colleague and also appears to be able to fit in routine visits more easily. On the other hand the attached H.V. has more consultations with the G.P. and spends more time with him than does her counterpart. The administrative load seems equally high in both schemes and there is no significant difference between the time of individual journeys although the aligned H.V. totals more travelling time due to the higher number of visits". (Poulton, 1977, Page 54).

8. Study No. 25—Naidoo (data: 1976)

Naidoo analysed the work of 11 health visitors in four teams in the same locality (Kentish Town, London). Teams A and B were attached and based in a health centre, Team C was not attached but was based in a health centre, and Team D was attached but was not based in a health centre. Highly significant (p = ·001) differences between the teams were found for most of the variables considered, but these "do not add up to a holistic account of C workers operating in a different way to other workers". After extensive and very careful computer analysis designed to search for factors which would explain the variance found, Naidoo found that "of all the factors looked at, 'team' was the most powerful, followed by marital status and dates of qualifications as S.R.N. and H.V.". Characteristics of the clientele being visited were eliminated as a prime source of differentiation—the difference was in the health visitors themselves. Naidoo concluded:

> "Team was the only factor to produce significant differences amongst all the variables looked at. This suggests that 'team' alone is powerful enough to produce distinct sub-populations of health visitors and their cases ... Reference group theory provides a rationale ... It is suggested that 'team' operates as a reference group for its members thus manipulating attitudes and behaviour to create a 'team image', a holistic approach to the functions of primary health care ... The hypothesis that is being advanced is that members learn to work efficiently with each other by taking the primary health care team as their reference group and adapting their ways of working to fit in with the goals and ideology of the team to which they belong". (Naidoo, 1977, Page 28).

9. Study No. 32—Walworth-Bell (data: 1978)

Walworth-Bell studied the work of 70 health visitors in two neighbouring health districts within the same area health authority in London. In one of the two districts the health visitors were attached, in the other they were mainly organised on a "patch" (i.e. geographical) basis. The study attempted to examine the effect of the organisational system on three aspects of the health visitor's work—namely "overall cover", "specific cover" and "function"—by hypothesising significant differences in the visits recorded by the health visitors in the two districts.

No difference was found in "function", but differences were found in "overall cover" and "specific cover", with some of the advantages claimed for either "patch" or "attachment" confirmed, and others contradicted. There was no difference in the variety of reasons for visiting, nor in the age range covered, or in the type of visit. The health visitors in the "patch" area recorded more visits per health visitor (but the difference disappears when the figures are corrected to take account of the number of sessions available for visiting), more visits which took place in the street, more very short visits, more visits to families known not to have a G.P., more visits "initiated by no-one" and fewer visits initiated by G.P.s. In all these cases, however, the numbers were exceedingly small, both in absolute terms and as percentages. In the two client groups considered in "specific cover", namely new births and persons aged over 75 years, no difference was found in the case of new births, and the difference found in the case of the elderly was in the direction opposite to that expected (i.e. the coverage in the "patch" area was greater) and this was explained by the employment in this district of geriatric health visitors.

Quite apart from the differences in the organisation of the health visiting service, there are considerable differences in the social structure of the two districts, some of which are taken into account; differences in the H.V.: population ratio are not mentioned.

In addition to these studies which are primarily concerned with the effects of attachment, four other studies also offer some further information. Henderson (Study No. 19) took as her study population all the health visitors in Hampshire, the vast majority of whom were working within attachment schemes; she did, however, note differences in the work of attached health visitors in Portsmouth compared with that of the non-attached health visitors in the same town. Watson (Study No. 33) studied 21 volunteer health visitors, 12 of whom were attached, five of whom worked a traditional geographical district, and the remaining four a combination of the two. Clark (Study No. 8) described the health visitor's home visits in an area where all the health visitors were attached to general practices, but included in her report a separate analysis of the 150 visits which were initiated by the general practitioner and compared them with the visits initiated by the client and those initiated by the health visitor herself. Marris (Study No. 22) found that the number of health visitors who were attached either to a general practice or to some combination of general practice and geographic area was small (42 out of 215 in his sample), but some of his data are presented separately for the different groups.

The findings of these thirteen studies can now be drawn together under the six headings:

Allocation of time to various activities; clientele; travel; consultation and communication with G.P.s; referrals; content/orientation of work.

1. Allocation of Time to Various Activities

Differences reported by all the studies are slight and probably not statistically significant. The only activity in which a change is consistently reported is consultation with general practitioners. Since the total time available is fixed (100 per cent), it is inevitable that as the proportion of time allocated to one activity increases the proportion of time available for other activities must be decreased. In absolute terms, however, if time allocated to one activity is increased, and the commitment to certain other activities is fixed (e.g. clinic sessions) the reduction must show in those activities which are susceptible to flexibility—for example, home visiting—and clerical work. Allen and King (Study No. 2) could find no difference except that the time spent in child health sessions was greater in both years in Hemel Hempstead as this included time spent with G.P.s some of whom conducted their own child health clinics. Ambler (Study No. 4) and Marris (Study No. 22) both reported that slightly more time was spent by attached health visitors on home visiting than by non-attached and slightly less on clerical work. Clow (Study No. 9) and Watson (Study No. 33) on the other hand found that the attached health visitors spent slightly less time on visiting. Poulton (Study No. 29) could find no significant difference.

2. Clientele

The studies show a slight but consistent shift from routine visits to small children towards visits to the elderly. Allen and King (Study No. 2) found that in St. Albans in 1966 when the health visitor became attached there was a slight fall in visits to the under fives, but that the proportion was still higher than the proportion recorded in Hemel Hempstead by 5 per cent. In both areas there was an increased proportion of visits to the elderly and for social problems not specified, and an overall increase in work with the elderly, mentally ill, disabled and social problems— markedly in St. Albans in 1966 from 4·4 per cent to 9 per cent and in Hemel Hempstead from 11·1 per cent to 13·6 per cent.

Ambler *et al* (Study No. 4) reported that the number of visits in which the welfare of children under five was discussed was 65 per cent in the attached town compared with 82 per cent and 90 per cent in the other two towns, while the number in which the welfare of elderly people was discussed was 18 per cent in the attached town compared with 10 per cent and 5 per cent in the other two.

Clow (Study No. 9) found that visits to expectant mothers and under fives constituted 54 per cent of the visits undertaken by attached health visitors compared with 58 per cent of the visits undertaken by non-attached health visitors (both groups are considerably lower than the proportion recorded by other studies: see Chapter 4). In this case, however, the attached health visitors also undertook fewer visits to the elderly, but Clow suggests that the figure for this group are distorted by the differences in the organisation of home help supervision.

Graham (Study No. 18) reported a range of 33 per cent to 38 per cent of visits made to children under five by attached health visitors compared with a range of 50 per cent to 81 per cent for non-attached health visitors, and a range of 32 per cent to 48 per cent for visits to the elderly made by attached health visitors compared with 10 per cent to 31 per cent by non-attached health visitors.

Marris (Study No. 22) reported that the proportion of time which attached health visitors spent dealing with mothers and babies differed little from the average but the time devoted to children was certainly less, while they spent roughly twice as much time with elderly as the non-attached health visitors (3·4 per cent, compared with 1·7 per cent). Marris comments:

"Generalising, we can say that the pattern of their work was less concentrated on the young and spread more evenly over the population as a whole". (Marris, 1971, Page 25).

Dawtrey (Study No. 10) found that the "origin of contact" in the case records of the attached health visitor was birth notification in 55·2 per cent of cases, an elderly person in 13·8 per cent, and "other" in 31 per cent. The proportions for the non-attached health visitor were 81·5 per cent, 7·4 per cent and 11·1 per cent respectively.

Poulton (Study No. 29) found no significant difference in the number of visits per day to the elderly or to families, but noted that the aligned health visitors made "significantly more" (no figures given) routine visits to babies and toddlers than the attached health visitors:

"They represent 21·8 per cent of the total number of visits but it appears that at least in our sample they were almost all made by H.V.s in alignment and have, in fact, been made on 50 per cent of alignment days, mostly arising from two units". (Poulton, 1977, Page 48).

The ambiguity is probably due to the inadequacy of Poulton's category system which confused age groups (e.g. baby, toddler) with purpose (e.g. routine, family support). Similarly, Henderson (Study No. 19) reported that:

"There were differences (significant at p.02) in the number of visits carried out for the purpose of advising on child management between those who worked a geographical caseload in Portsmouth and those who worked a G.P. caseload in Portsmouth". (Henderson, 1977, Page 41).

The data reported by Clark (Study No. 8) differ from that of the other studies because all the health visitors in her sample were attached and, therefore, no comparison with non-attached health visitors was possible.

However, the analysis of the visits which were initiated by the general practitioner showed a very different clientele from the visits which were initiated by the health visitor herself. Clark reported:

"The groups which the general practitioner asked the health visitor to visit were in general those with which the non-attached health visitor has little contact. Just over 60 per cent of the visits initiated by the general practitioner were to families where there were no young children, while the greater majority (77·5 per cent) of the visits initiated by the health visitor herself were to families where there were young children. The proportion of visits to the elderly was almost three times as great among visits initiated by the general practitioner as among visits initiated by the health visitor herself. Moreover, in 40 per cent of the visits initiated by the general practitioner, the health visitor has not previously visited the family, compared with 16·4 per cent of visits initiated by the health visitor; in 60 cases the G.P. has put the health visitor in touch with a problem which she would probably not otherwise have known about". (Clark, 1973, Page 84).

3. Travel

It has frequently been suggested that an increase in the amount of travelling time is an inevitable consequence of attachment to general practices and that this is one of the major disadvantages of the policy. In fact this is not borne out by the evidence of the studies in this review. Allen and King (Study No. 2), Ambler (Study No. 4) and Graham (Study No. 18) found no significant differences in the time spent on travelling by attached and non-attached health visitors. Clow (Study No. 9) reported that "Strangely enough, this was slightly greater in the unattached group, although the mileage covered by the attached nurses was nearly 400 miles greater (2,113 against 1,726)". Similarly, Poulton (Study No. 29) reported that "there is no significant difference between the time of individual journeys, although the aligned H.V. totals more travelling time due to the higher number of visits". Marris found that health visitors working in geographic areas spent 9·9 per cent of their time on travelling, attached health visitors 11·9 per cent, and those working in a combination system spent 13·5 per cent.

4. Consultation and Communication with G.P.s

Not surprisingly, all studies report increased consultation and communication with G.P.s when the health visitor is attached to general practice. Of Clark's sample of 78 health visitors in an area where all the health visitors were attached, all but one had been in contact with the general practitioner during the previous week. Allen and King (Study No. 2) reported that the average daily time spent on consultation with the G.P. increased from one minute to six in St. Albans; the daily time in Hemel Hempstead was 12 minutes in 1965 and eight minutes in 1966. Ambler et al (Study No. 4) reported that the health visitors in Town A had much more contact with G.P.s than the health visitors in the other two towns. The attached H.V.s spent longer in general practice clinics and in meetings with G.P.s; they also communicated about more families with the doctors (on average 10 communications per week compared with 4·5 for liaison health visitors and 0·5 for geographically based health visitors). Half of the communications about families in Town A were initiated by the G.P.s themselves and most (80 per cent) of them took the form of face-to-face discussions.

Clow (Study No. 9) reported that attached health visitors spent on average two hours eight minutes each week on liaison with colleagues and visits to general practitioners' surgeries, compared with their non-attached colleagues' one hour. Poulton (Study No. 29) found that the differences, both on time and in the frequency of communications, were significant at the level of p.05. Watson (Study No. 33) found that the attached health visitors who worked from a surgery base spent on average ten minutes per day in face-to-face communication with G.P.s, attached nurses who worked from a clinic base spent five minutes, health visitors who had a combination of attachment and district spent one minute, and the health visitors who worked entirely on a district basis spent no time at all on communication with G.P.s.

5. Referrals

Referral patterns as distinct from communication or consultation are reported in six of these 13 studies (Nos. 2, 8, 9, 10, 25 and 32). Further information is also available from Allen, King and Abbott (Study No. 3), Gilmore (Study No. 16) and Gilmore et al (Study No. 17).

Allen and King (Study No. 2) reported that the number of referrals from G.P.s to H.V.s in St. Albans increased considerably after attachment, especially referrals of adults which increased from 0·4 per month to 4·1 per month. Referrals also increased in Hemel Hempstead where the attachment was longer established. The number of referrals to social workers also increased. Allen and King remark, however, that:

"the comparison of the number of referrals was not easy as health visitors and general medical practitioners vary in their method of working, which led to difficulty in comparing the number of referrals made by individual health visitors and doctors". (Allen and King, 1968, Page 179.)

Table 13, which showed the source or initiation of visits as reported in eight studies, showed that the proportion of the health visitor's visits which were initiated by the G.P. ranged from 1·8 per cent (Study No. 3) to 43·3 per cent (Study No. 16). Walworth-Bell (Study No. 32) reported that 6 per cent of visits were initiated by G.P.s in the "attached" district compared with 2 per cent in the "patch" district. Gilmore et al (Study No. 17) reported that 34 per cent of the health visitors' visits were initiated by the general practitioner in Centre A, 15 per cent in Centre B, and 17 per cent in Centre C. They discuss their findings in relation to their earlier study (and report that for the earlier study, if re-visits are included, the proportion of visits initiated by the G.P. is reduced to 19 per cent) and also in relation to those of Clark. Clark suggested that if a "high" proportion of the health visitor's work was initiated by the G.P. this might suggest that the health visitor was acting "less as an independent practitioner and more as an agent of the G.P.". She felt that Gilmore's 43 per cent was probably "too high" while 7·3 per cent was not high enough to pose such a threat, but remarked that:

"The 'right' level of referral is difficult to determine. In the end, however, it is the responsibility of the health visitor to determine her own priorities in visiting whatever referrals she receives; the extent to which the G.P. directs her work is a function of her own conception of her role and her confidence in herself as an independent practitioner". (Clark, 1973, Page 82.)

Gilmore et al quote this remark and confirm Clark's view:

"As there are no criteria available for determining the 'appropriate' levels of referral it is impossible to decide if those recorded in Centres A, B and C are too high or too low. It may have to be left to the discretion of health visitors to decide which referrals to accept or reject". (Gilmore et al, 1974, Page 65.)

Contact with other agencies, including G.P.s, made by health visitors subsequent to client consultation was discussed in Chapter 11. However, while these figures would include referrals, they may also include communications which did not lead to referral. Allen and King (Study No. 2) specifically report referrals: referrals of children by the health visitor to the G.P. in St. Albans rose from 1·5 per month to 3·3 per month, and referrals of adults from 1·0 to 1·4; in Hemel Hempstead where the H.V.s were attached throughout the figures were 2·3 and 1·9 for children and 3·4 and 4·7 for adults. Dawtrey (Study No. 10) reported that 1·7 per cent of the attached health visitor's cases were referred to "G.P. or hospital", compared with the non-attached health visitor's 7·4 per cent. However, the data are too small and too imprecise for any conclusions to be drawn. Walworth-Bell (Study No. 32) reported that 13·8 per cent of visits were followed by referral to the G.P. in the "attached" district compared with nine per cent in the "patch" district.

6. Content/Orientation of Work

The general "broadening" of the health visitor's work in attachment schemes which was specifically noted by Allen and King (Study No. 2) has already been described in terms of the clientele of the visit. Walworth-Bell (Study No. 32), Poulton (Study No. 29) and Watson (Study No. 33) found no differences in work content between attached health visitors and others. Ambler et al (Study No. 4), however, reported:

"Health visitors in Town A also recorded that a higher percentage of the families they visited had special health and social characteristics. Special health problems were present in 50 per cent of the visits in Town A compared with 36 per cent and 29 per cent of visits in the district towns. . . . In Town A the H.V.s discussed an illness or its treatment (i.e. a curative topic) on 47 per cent of visits, compared to 38 per cent and 34 per cent in the district towns.... Critics of attachment schemes have suggested that a danger of attaching H.V.s to general practices would be that the H.V.s would lose their interest in preventive health. It is, therefore, particularly interesting that discussion of curative topics in Town A was an addition to rather than a replacement of preventive work". (Ambler *et al*, 1968, Page 298.)

They remark, however, "This may have been due to working in general practice attachments but we can produce no evidence which proves this". Watson (Study No. 33) specifically noted that there was no difference between attached and other health visitors in the percentage of visits in which "illness" was the main topic group discussed.

Clark (Study No. 8) also discussed the suggestion that attachment results in a tendency for the health visitor to move from preventive into curative work. Comparing the topics discussed in visits initiated by the general practitioner with those discussed in visits initiated by the health visitor, she found a higher incidence of discussion of general family health, specific illness or disability, home help, adjustment to illness, diet, emotional problems of adults, mental illness, bereavement, and social security benefits. When the topics were grouped into the broad categories of "physical health", "mental health" and "social care", there was a lower proportion of topics concerned with physical health and a higher proportion of topics concerned with the psycho-social aspects of health than in the sample as a whole. She concluded that "This suggests that where the health visitor is dealing with sick people and their illnesses, she tends to concentrate on the social and emotional aspects of the illness. (Clark, 1973, Page 85.)

Discussion

This review of the data reported by 13 studies concerning the effect of attachment on the work of the health visitor suggests that:

(a) the differences reported are small, and
(b) such differences as are found cannot conclusively be attributed to attachment.

As Clark (1973) suggested in relation to her own data:

"The findings ... do not confirm either the fears expressed by those who oppose attachment schemes, or all the hopes of the policy's most ardent supporters".

The difficulty of attributing the differences reported to attachment is particularly great: correlation does not necessarily imply causation. Ambler *et al* (Study No. 4), who found quite large differences in a number of variables, specifically remarked "while it has been possible to show that the patterns of work were different, it is much more difficult to demonstrate that any differences have been caused by attachment". There is, however, some evidence about other factors which are also

85

related to differences in clientele and patterns of work. Clark (Study No. 8) and Henderson (Study No. 19) have demonstrated a strong relationship between work patterns and the date of qualification; Ambler *et al* (Study No. 4) and Henderson (Study No. 19) have pointed to the effect of staffing levels; the studies of Gilmore (Study No. 16) in Brighton, and Graham (Study No. 18) in Worthing point to the effect of the population structure of the area in which the study is located; Naidoo (Study No. 25) has suggested the importance of the team as a reference group; Watson (Study No. 33) and Graham (Study No. 18) indicate the extent of individual variation in work patterns.

Probably the most important variable is in fact the passage of time. Discussing the limitations of conceptualising nursing in terms of tasks, Schlotfeldt (1975) writes:

"The first of these (limitations) is the assumption of constancy in what practitioners do. With advances in knowledge and technology and by agreement among practitioners, those with whom they work and those they serve, practices change remarkably over time. Indeed, some activities become obsolete as concepts of health care change and as new knowledge, techniques, therapies, devices, instruments and services become available for practitioners' use". (Schlotfeldt, 1975, Pages 11–12.)

The decade during which most of these studies have been undertaken has been a period of considerable and rapid change in health visiting. Quite apart from the introduction of attachment schemes, there has been a broadening of the prescribed role of the health visitor which has been made quite explicit in changes in the syllabus of training and in the policies of central government and local employing authorities. The concept of the multidisciplinary team and the team approach to health care has also developed during this period and has been shown by Reedy (1977) and others to be a phenomenon which is distinct from the development of attachment schemes. There have been changes in the scope and organisation of health and social services. Without control of such obvious intervening variables as these (and such control would be very difficult to achieve) differences in work patterns cannot be attributed directly to attachment. It is disturbing that such flimsy "evidence" is accorded so much weight by both the supporters and opponents of attachment schemes, for, as I have pointed out before:

"The mere fact of attachment does not change the health visitor's work in any way; her potential clientele is the same, whether people are listed according to the street in which they live or according to their general practitioner, and her statutory duties remain unchanged. Any changes in clientele are the result of decisions which must be made jointly by doctors and nurses about which vulnerable groups ought to be followed up and what machinery needs to be devised to enable this to be done. Any change in emphasis in work content and the extent to which the health visitor allows her work to be directed by the general practitioner is the responsibility of the health visitor herself. Attachment does not create the changes; it merely provides the opportunity". (Clark, 1973, Page 86.)

CHAPTER 13

Where Do We Go From Here?

Discussing her review of over sixty studies relating to attrition among student and pupil nurses, Jillian MacGuire wrote:

> "What does emerge from a comprehensive overview of the literature is that so many individual projects seem to have been carried out without much reference to any previous work either in the fields of nursing, of general education, or of large scale organisations. There is little or no sense in the accumulation of information or the growth of understanding. Work in this field suffers from the pragmatism endemic in the British approach to the social survey which tends to regard theories with suspicion and facts as self-explanatory". (MacGuire, 1969, Page 121.)

This review was, to some extent, modelled on that of MacGuire; and the reviewer's conclusion is exactly the same. While the collection of data presented in this review is interesting for its own sake, and should at least dispose of the often-repeated myth that "nothing is known about the work of health visitors", its usefulness, particularly for strategic planning purposes, is limited.

Many of the limitations of these studies are, in fact, limitations inherent in social surveys, which would not be overcome by the use of larger samples or the provision of greater resources of time, skill or money. For example, demonstration of the causal relationships which are implicit in objectives such as "to assess the effect of attachment on the work of the health visitor" is extraordinarily difficult; and the demonstration of correlations is of little value unless control of important variables such as staffing levels, local management policies, the age and training of the health visitor, and many other factors can be achieved.

There are, however, two areas of information which are susceptible to survey methods and where the data presently available are inadequate. These are the health visitor's clientele and the organisational pattern of home visits. One reason for the inadequacy of the data, as discussed in Chapter 2, is the failure to develop proper category systems. The development of a standardised category system for clientele and for factors such as source of referral is crucial not only for further research but also for use in routine health visiting records.

Records are not themselves research, but they must be able to provide essential background information if research effort is not to be wasted on the collection and sifting of basic data, and they are also necessary to provide sound sampling frames for specific pieces of research. Moreover, health visiting records provide the on-going information which alone can document changes over time and which alone, therefore, can show the effect of policy changes such as attachment or early hospital discharge or changes in legislation or the emergence of "new" problems such as child abuse.

The present deplorable state of health visiting records is perhaps shown by the following extract from the work of Dawtrey, who was herself not a health visitor and who was clearly surprised by what she found:

"The Area Health Authority would not give permission for a detailed survey of health visitors' records at Health Centre B, because of a previous experience of loss of confidentiality. But access was given to the weekly returns made by all the health visitors to the Health Authority. These returns do not give much detailed information and after studying several months of returns, it was found that each health visitor interpreted them differently. (The format of the weekly returns had changed during the previous year and become considerably more complicated.) Although there had been discussions regarding the filling in of these new forms, the system was not sufficiently well established to obtain reliable information from them. Apart from the fact that the health visitors did not completely understand them, the returns were also regarded as 'the weekly liar', a term actually used. No deliberate attempt was made to give misinformation but the aims and objectives were unclear. Consequently, the forms were not completed regularly. The health visitors did them in batches and often could not remember precisely what had happened on visits and in clinic sessions. The health visitors' diaries gave the minimum of detail and might not include casual meetings in the street or unsuccessful visits. It was concluded that no reliable data could be derived from weekly returns and any hope of obtaining statistical data from the health centre was abandoned. These weekly returns are used for government statistics on the health visiting service and provide another example for the health visitor of tiresome and apparently pointless form-filling all so common in the social welfare bureaucracies". (Dawtrey, 1977, Pages 39-40.)

Health visiting work comprises two main activities: verbal interaction and decision making. The analysis of verbal interaction depends on direct recording by the use of either observers or tape recorders or both; work in this field is currently being undertaken by the author. Decision making has been studied in other fields and it is likely that methods used for the analysis of decision making in other fields could be applied to the study of decision making in health visiting. For example, carefully prepared interviews conducted by skilled interviewers with a sample of health visitors, perhaps related to the health visitor's previous day's visits, could yield extremely useful information about the factors involved in the decision to visit, the objectives of the visit, how health visitors plan their work and set priorities, and more detailed information about clientele (such as the nature of the problems identified) than could be obtained by questionnaires or work schedules.

Time studies, which are part of the field of work study, are quite outside the scope of the social survey altogether. The difficulties of self-timing were discussed in Chapter 3. One major difficulty, namely the need to stop doing the activity in order to write something about it on a recording schedule, could be to a considerable extent overcome by the use of tape recorders as in Study No. 7 (City of Leicester 1969). It is perhaps unfortunate that this study was not published, because if its methodological approach had been more widely known it might have been more widely adopted.

A few areas of health visiting activity are susceptible to observational work study techniques which have been used and validated in many other fields. Two areas which have been shown by this review to need further attention and which should be susceptible to these techniques are clinic work and clerical work. It is likely that a study of either of these areas, using observational work study techniques, would provide information which would be useful for planning the best use of resources, both in terms of improving the health visitor's own efficiency and for the delegation of some tasks to other personnel.

It is clear that no one method can produce an adequate description of health visiting activity; a variety of methods must be used in combination. The application of a particular method to a field for which it is inappropriate produces a picture which is at best incomplete, at worst hopelessly distorted. Unfortunately, this has happened all too often in health visiting research to date.

Better descriptive research in health visiting, conducted with greater methodological rigour than is shown by the studies included in this review, is badly needed. Since the variation in health visiting activity has been shown to be very great, comparative studies are also needed. For example, no study has so far been carried out to compare the work of health visitors in an area where caseloads are high with the work in a (socially and geographically) similar area where the recommended health visitor : population ratio (DHSS Circular 47/72) has been achieved; the variation in activity found by Henderson (Study No. 19) between health districts with differing ratios within a single AHA suggests that further study might produce interesting and useful results.

However, the limitations of descriptive research must be recognised. As Hicks (1976) remarked:

"All this is interesting, but it is a bit like counting the rivets in the Queen Mary, which would tell us nothing about how well she functions". (Hicks, 1976, Page 265.)

The description of tasks, moreover, is in itself of limited value; it adds nothing, as Schlotfeldt (1975) has pointed out, to understanding practice, to evaluating practice, or to the knowledge base of practice. It shows only what is currently being done, not what is not being done; it cannot, therefore, be used to estimate need, either patients' needs or staffing needs. It is a measure of quantity not quality. Time studies are similarly limited and should be used only for specific purposes. In discussing their uses and limitations Arnstein (1956) remarks:

"Time studies are not an end in themselves. They have to have a reason when they are started and an action programme is anticipated following the study. A time study is not ordinarily one of the research projects that you do to add to the sum of human knowledge; you do it because something is wrong and this is one method of getting information for correcting it". (Arnstein, 1956, Page 28.)

It is perhaps significant that while one of the earliest nursing research projects undertaken in the United States was an analysis of the work of public health nurses (Committee for the Study of Nursing Education 1923), and a number of studies similar to those contained in this review appeared in the American nursing literature during the 1950s and 1960s, more recent studies have attempted to analyse the process of nursing and to relate it to some kind of conceptual framework. In the study of health visiting this kind of research has barely begun.

Two of the studies included in this review, however, have attempted to go further than simple description. Wiseman (Study No. 35) and Walworth-Bell (Study No. 29) have attempted to match health visiting activity to health visiting "need" as defined by the prevalence in a given population of certain "vulnerable groups". Walworth-Bell limited this part of her study to the "specific cover" of two groups within the population—new babies and elderly people aged over 75 years—which are widely accepted as being "vulnerable" or "in need of health visiting" and are also fairly readily identifiable within existing record systems. Wiseman's study was more ambitious in that it "involves developing a model which will provide target visiting rates for each health visitor such that sector targets will be achieved and the pattern of visiting for each individual health visitor is in line with her interests and priorities" (Wiseman, 1979, Page 97), and also because it includes many more "vulnerable groups" (26 "care groups") and incorporates the multiple perspectives of the practitioners and the managers as well as the demographic data itself.

"Activity data of the health visitors' contacts and functions to the care groups will help the managers to monitor both the health visitors' variation from the managerial target objectives as well as the variations from the health visitors' subjective judgements of health visiting priorities. By taking the various aspects of the research data into account, the nurse managers will be able to allocate care group target objectives to the health visitors which both conform to the community's need and the health visitors' interests and priority judgements. Thus, it is envisaged that the nurse managers will be assisted towards directing health visiting effort which conforms with the current day preventive health care needs and which will help to guarantee the provision of an effective health visiting service to the community". (Wiseman, 1979, Page 104.)

The method clearly needs careful testing and the tools probably require further refinement, but the concept does offer a way of tackling the problem of determining appropriate staffing levels in health visiting.

It is important to recognise that this concept is quite different from that of the "performance targets" sugested by Gallaher *et al* (Study No. 13) and Young (Study No. 37). The "performance targets" are based on the concept of using the mean recorded time for a particular task (in this case a health visitor's home visit) as an ideal "target" time. Young (1971) suggests:

> "Such target times can thus be estimated for each health visiting activity, if each nurse records weekly the number and type of visits and clinics she carried out, the administrative staff can estimate a weekly target time for each nurse. If the nurse also records her actual weekly time on duty, the weekly target time expressed as a percentage of the actual weekly time can be returned to each nurse as her performance ratio for that week. . . . The performance ratios could engender a spirit of competition among the members of a nursing group, but there is no harm in this. As far as the administrative staff is concerned the ratios would provide a measure of overall nursing performance". (Young, 1971, Page 161.)

The notion that "number of visits" should be used as a measure of health visiting performance is not likely to be acceptable to health visitors because it undermines the concepts of clinical freedom and individualised care. Gallaher *et al* noted that the idea was at first resisted but finally accepted; the conclusion to the booklet which they issued to staff is perhaps significant:

> "We feel that in time, if you give it a fair trial, you will come to prefer working in a controlled situation. And this is *not* to imply that chaos reigned before O and M came upon the scene. On the contrary, your work has always been subject to controls. All we are trying to do is to formalise them and express them in a way which can enable you to work more effectively. . . . And, finally, from a selfish, professional point of view, we in Work Study and O & M want them to work. Because when on some future assignment a Chief Officer or a supervisor or a Trade Union Official tells us 'It won't work here—you cannot control this type of work' we can point to you. We can say in all honesty that if district nurses and health visitors can make it work in *their* jobs, it will work anywhere. So you may be making a much bigger contribution to increased productivity than any of us realise".

Gallaher's report that the establishment of performance targets was followed by an increase of 38 per cent in the amount of visiting (without any change in clinic and school sessions), taken in conjunction with Dawtrey's comments on the "weekly liar" (page 97), perhaps demonstrates the naivety of this approach.

The evaluation of health visiting activity poses quite separate problems and demands quite different methods of study. The problems are not only methodological but conceptual also. The classic model of evaluation involves the measurement of the specific effect of a specific variable on outcome. For example, most clinical medical research is concerned with measuring the effect of a specified therapy (e.g. a defined amount of a particular drug) on a measurable outcome (e.g. mortality). In health visiting the choice of appropriate outcomes and the ability to attribute a particular outcome to a particular intervention are highly problematical and need careful study. At a more basic level, even, the "specific variable" which may relatively easily be defined in other fields of research (e.g. a measured amount of a particular drug or a particular surgical procedure) is much more difficult to define in health visiting. This is one reason why better descriptive research in health visiting is needed; until the "specific variable" which health visiting practice constitutes is accurately described and analysed, evaluation of its effectiveness is extremely difficult.

One small-scale study which attempts to evaluate one aspect of health visiting activity (specific intervention by a health visitor with a group of elderly people) is known to be currently in progress (Luker 1978). Current work by the author in this review includes a search for indicators which might be developed as evaluative criteria to be used in future research. One study included in the present review, however, highlights, perhaps unwittingly, the pitfalls of the task. Walworth-Bell (Study No. 32), in attempting to assess whether health visiting was more "effective" when the health visitors were attached to general practice than when they were geographically organised, assumed that "effectiveness" could be measured by measuring the health knowledge of parents of first-born nine-month-old children in the following fields: immunisation, child development, emergencies, contraception and smoking. She found not only that there was no difference between the two districts, but, perhaps more importantly, that the level of parents' knowledge in all fields was very scanty, that parents did not necessarily perceive the contribution of the health visitor as relevant to their knowledge in these fields, that parents knew very little about the health visitor's function at all. While the findings should in themselves be a matter for concern to health visitors, they also show the difficulties involved in choosing apparently "obvious" outcome criteria, in measuring them once chosen, and in attributing particular outcomes (or lack of them) to particular interventions. To continue the analogy of drug evaluation, it would be tempting but misleading to suggest that aspirin was ineffective as a treatment for headache as a result of an experiment in which the dosage was limited to 5mg and the headache was caused by a brain tumour.

APPENDIX A

STUDIES OF THE WORK OF THE HEALTH VISITOR:
BIBLIOGRAPHIC DETAILS

1. AKESTER, J. M. AND MCPHAIL, A. (1963). *Health Visiting in the Sixties.* London, Macmillan (*Nursing Times* Publication).
2. ALLEN, W. H. AND KING, V. M. (1968). A Study of Health Visitor Attachment to General Practitioners in Hertfordshire. *Medical Officer,* **119**, 13, 177 (reprinted in *Nursing Times* Occasional Papers 15 November 1968, 177–179).
3. ALLEN, W. H., KING, V. M. AND ABBOTT, G. M. (1969). *Domiciliary Nursing Services in Hertfordshire.* Part I: Health Visitors. Hertfordshire County Council. Unpublished report.
4. AMBLER, M. *et al* (1968). The Attachment of Local Health Authority Staff to General Practice. *Medical Officer,* **119**, 13, 295–299.
5. ATKINSON, M. B. (1971). Survey into the Work of the Health Visitor. *Health in the West Riding* 1971, 13–19.
6. CARTER, F. (1973). *The Activities of General Practice.* Department of Engineering Production, University of Birmingham. M.Sc. report. Unpublished.
7. CITY OF LEICESTER (1969). *Survey of Health Visiting Services.* Town Clerk's Department, Management Services Branch, Town Hall, Leicester. (Assignment S/I; Project HV1.) Unpublished report.
8. CLARK, M. J. (1972). *The Work of the Health Visitor.* University of Reading, M.Phil thesis. Unpublished.
8a. CLARK, M. J. (1973). *A Family Visitor. A Descriptive Analysis of Health Visiting in Berkshire.* London, Royal College of Nursing.
8b. CLARK, M. J. (1972). What Do Health Visitors Do? *Nursing Times* (Occasional Papers), **68**, 30, 117–119.
8c. CLARK, M. J. (1972). The "New Breed" Health Visitor. *Nursing Times* (Occasional Papers), **68**, 31, 121–122.
8d. CLARK, M. J. (1972). The Effect of Attachment on the Work of the Health Visitor. *Nursing Times* (Occasional Papers), **68**, 31, 123–124.
8e. CLARK, M. J. (1976). The Role of the Health Visitor: A Study Conducted in Berkshire, England. *Journal of Advanced Nursing,* **1**, 25–36.
9. CLOW, J. T. (1968). Attachment of Health Visitors to General Practitioners. *Medical Officer,* **119**, 13, 173 (reprinted in *Nursing Times* Occasional Papers 8 October 1968, 161–164).
10. DAWTREY, E. (1977). *The Health Visitor in Primary Care.* Medical Architecture Research Unit, North London Polytechnic. M.Sc. report. Unpublished.
11. ELLWOOD, M. AND JEFFERYS, M. (1976). In: Hicks, D. (1976) *Primary Health Care* (285–288). London, H.M.S.O.
12. FRY, J., DILLANE, J. B. AND CONOLLY, M. (1965). The Evolution of a Health Team: A Successful G.P.—H.V. Association. *British Medical Journal,* **i**, 181.
13. GALLAHER, E., HOWE, J., MCNEIL, A., RICHARDSON, E. AND ROSS, A.

(1970). A Study of Health Visiting and District Nursing in Bolton. *Medical Officer,* 27 March, 1970.

14. GETTINGS, B. (1970). Health Visiting Needs in General Practice. *Health Visitor,* 1971, **44,** 9, 285–288.

15. GETTINGS, B. (1971). A School Nursing Work Study in Berkshire. *Health Visitor,* **44,** 9, 285–288.

16. GILMORE, M. (1970). A Pilot Study of the Work of the Nursing Team in General Practice. *Medical Officer,* **124,** 18, 238–243.

17. GILMORE, M., BRUCE, N. AND HUNT, M. (1974). *The Work of the Nursing Team in General Practice.* London, Council for the Education and Training of Health Visitors.

18. GRAHAM, J. A. G. (1966). A Health Visitor Work Study. *Medical Officer,* **116,** 27.

19. HENDERSON, J. (1977). *Health Visiting in Hampshire.* University of Surrey M.Sc. Dissertation. (Unpublished.)

19a. HENDERSON, J. (1978). What do Health Visitors Do? *Nursing Mirror,* 14 September, 30–32.

20. JEFFERYS, M. (1965). *An Anatomy of Social Welfare Services.* London, Michael Joseph.

21. LOVELAND, M. (1969). *A Survey of the Work of Health Visitors in an Urban and a Rural Area.* University of Surrey, M.Phil. thesis. Unpublished.

22. MARRIS, T. (1971). *The Work of Health Visitors in London.* London, Greater London Council (Department of Planning and Transportation. Research Report No. 12).

23. MINISTRY OF HEALTH, DEPARTMENT OF HEALTH FOR SCOTLAND, AND MINISTRY OF EDUCATION (1956). *An Enquiry Into Health Visiting: Report of the Working Party on the Field of Work, Training and Recruitment of Health Visitors* (Chairman: Sir W. Jameson). London, H.M.S.O.

24. MORRIS, M. E. (1976). *Health Visiting Survey.* Preston Health District. Unpublished report.

25. NAIDOO, J. (1977). *A Preliminary Analysis of the Visiting Patterns of Attached and Non-attached Health Visitors.* Social Research Unit, Bedford College, University of London. Unpublished report.

26. NIMMO, A. W. (1979). *A Survey of Child Health Clinics at the Denburn Health Centre, Aberdeen.* Report No. 37. Operational Research Group, Grampian Health Services Information Unit. Grampian Health Board.

27. NIMMO, A. W. (1979). *A Survey of Child Health Clinics at Seaton Clinic, Aberdeen.* Report No. 39. Operational Research Group, Grampian Health Services Information Unit. Grampian Health Board.

28. POTTON, R. (1978). *Health Visitor Work Content Survey.* Kent Area Health Authority. Unpublished report.

28a. POTTON, R. (1977). *Health Visitor Work-Load Survey.* Tunbridge Wells Health District. Unpublished report.

28b. POTTON, R. (1978). *Health Visitor Work Content Survey.* Canterbury and Thanet Health District. Unpublished report.

28c. POTTON, R. (1978). *Health Visitor Work Content Survey.* South East Kent Health District. Unpublished report.

29. POULTON, K. (1977). *Evaluation of Community Nursing Service of Wandsworth and East Merton Teaching District.* Wandsworth and East Merton Health District. Unpublished report.

30. THORPE, E. C. (1978). *A Report on the Clerical Systems Relating to the Health Visitors at the Northcote Health Clinic, Ealing.* North West Thames Regional Health Authority. Unpublished.

31. THURMOTT, P. (1976). *Health and the School.* London, Royal College of Nursing.

32. WALWORTH-BELL, J. (1978). *Prospective Analysis of Health Visiting Work-load.* University of London, M.Sc. thesis. Unpublished.

32a. WALWORTH-BELL, J. (1979). Patch Work? *Health Visitor,* **52,** 8, 307–310.

33. WATSON, P. J. (1977). *A Time Study of Health Visiting.* Edinburgh, Scottish Home and Health Department. Unpublished report.

33a. WATSON, P. J. (1979). Studying Work. *Nursing Times* (Occasional Papers), **75,** 20, 81–84.

34. WHITE, W. (1972). *Survey and Analysis of the Work of the Health Visitor in Cardiff.* South Glamorgan Area Health Authority. Unpublished report.

35. WILKES, J. S. AND NIMMO, A. W. (1976). An Analysis of Work Patterns in Community Nursing. *Nursing Times* (Occasional Papers), 29 January 1976, pp. 13–16, and *Nursing Times* (Occasional Papers), 5 February 1976, pp. 17–20.

35a. WILKES, J. S. AND NIMMO, A. W. (1974). *Working Patterns in Community Nursing: An Analysis.* Report No. 20. Operational Research Group, North Eastern Health Services Research and Intelligence Unit. Grampian Health Board.

36. WISEMAN, J. (1979). *Health Visiting: The Allocation Problem of Health Visiting.* University of Lancaster, M.Sc. thesis. Unpublished.

36a. WISEMAN, J. (1979). Activities and Priorities of Health Visitors. *Nursing Times* (Occasional Papers), **75,** 24, 97–100 and **75,** 25, 101–104.

37. YOUNG, W. C. (1971). A Work Study of Nursing Staff in a Health Department. *Health Bulletin,* **29,** 3, 154–161.

APPENDIX B

SUMMARIES OF STUDIES OF THE WORK OF THE HEALTH VISITOR

The summaries are arranged in alphabetical order by the name of the researcher. All studies are summarised under the following headings:

1. Name of Researcher
2. Type of Project
3. Publications
4. Date of Study
5. Location of Study
6. Aims/Purpose of Study
7. Sample
8. Method
9. Main findings
10. Researcher's conclusions.

Studies marked with an asterisk (*) have been summarised by the reviewer. All other summaries have been prepared by the original researcher.

STUDY NO. 1*

Name of Researchers: Akester, J. M. and MacPhail, A. N.

Type of Project: Management survey (M.O.H. and Superintendent Health Visitor).

Publication: Akester, J. M. and MacPhail, A. N. (1963). Health Visiting in the Sixties. London. Macmillan (*Nursing Times* Publication).

Date of Study: 1961 (October).

Location: Leeds.

Aims/Purpose of Study: Not Specified.

Sample: All health visitors in Leeds except nine (sickness); days when health visitors were accompanied by a student not included; analysis based on 231 days worked by 51 health visitors.

Method: Health visitors were asked to record their work for one week using two forms:

(a) daily summary of time spent on different activities.

(b) form for each visit, showing type of visit, health visitor's findings, subsequent action and evaluation.

Main Findings:

(a) Allocation of time: see Tables 2, 3 and 4.

(b) *Visits:*

(1) One third were unexpected or "picked up" by the health visitor during the course of the day's work.

(2) The "poorer" homes were more frequently visited and these visits were time consuming.

(3) Seventy per cent of families visited had had no other visitor directly concerned with health during the preceding month.

(4) The health visitor assessed her reception as "cordial" in 87 per cent of visits, and felt that one per cent were unnecessary. Forty-two illustrative examples of home visits are given.

Researchers' Conclusions: Increasing numbers of elderly people and immigrant families will increase demands on the health visitor's time. Emphasises the importance of work "picked up" by the health visitor "on her beat".

Name of Researchers: Allen, W. M. and King, V. M.

Type of Project: Management survey (MOH and County Nursing Officer).

Publication: Allen, W. M. and King, V. M. (1968). A Study of Health Visitor Attachment to General Practitioners in Hertfordshire. *Nursing Times* (Occasional Papers) 15 November 1968, pp. 177–179.

Date of Study: 1965 (March) and 1966 (October).

Location: Hertfordshire (St. Albans and Hemel Hempstead).

Aims/Purpose of Study: Not Specified.

Sample: 1965: 10 health visitors in St. Albans—not attached.

13 health visitors in Hemel Hempstead—attached.

1966: 13 health visitors in St. Albans—attached prior to survey:

17 health visitors in Hemel Hempstead—attached throughout.

Records were kept for one month in each survey.

Method: The whole range of health visitors' duties was studied by a committee of nurse managers who designed the initial survey form. The survey forms, together with the usual monthly report forms, were completed by the health visitors for a month in each survey. The forms required a daily entry of work done, time spent, and communications made and received.

Main Findings:

Allocation of time: see Tables 2 and 3.

Average number of G.P.s with whom health visitors were working was 3·6 in Hemel Hempstead (attached throughout); in St. Albans the number was reduced from 27·5 to 3·6.

Clientele: 83 per cent of visits in St. Albans and 74 per cent in Hemel Hempstead were to children under five years.

Researchers' Conclusions: "the survey has shown that the range and amount of work carried out by the health visitors increased following attachment . . . that more time has been spent in consultation with G.P.s, and that more referrals took place between health visitors and G.P.s. The number of referrals made by health visitors to social workers also increased. . . . Travelling time and mileage were not found to increase significantly with the attachment schemes. . . . The survey has shown that there is a need for reducing time spent on clerical duties and administration.

STUDY NO. 3*

Name of Researchers: Allen, W. M., King, V. M. and Abbott, G. M.

Type of Project: Management survey (MOH, County Nursing officer and H.V. tutor).

Publication: Allen, W. M., King, V. M., and Abbott, G. M., Survey of Work Undertaken by Domiciliary Nurses in the County During February 1969. Unpublished report. Hertfordshire County Council.

Date of Study: 1969 (February).

Location: Hertfordshire.

Aims/Purpose of Study:

(1) To establish what exactly was the field of work of the health visitor, A.V. Asst., district nurse, midwife, and SEN district nurse, and their relationship to certain other agencies.

(2) To measure amount of time spent on specific services.

(3) To determine to what extent the duties of each nurse made full use of her professional skills.

Sample: All staff: 143 full-time health visitors, plus 26 triple-duty nurses (nine WTE) plus five specialist (TB) health visitors.

Response rate not given.

Records were kept for one month.

Method: "All staff completed a general questionnaire, a daily work analysis, a daily time analysis and the normal monthly report form. The forms were completed during the month of February 1969. A pilot study to validate the forms had previously been carried out and all staff attended meetings where the purposes of the study and the use of the forms were fully explained".

Main Findings:

Allocation of time: see Table 2.

Type of visit (clientele): see Table 7.

Proportion of "no reply" visits: 15·6 per cent.

Access to G.P. records: 20 per cent had no access, 39 per cent partial access, 40 per cent full access.

Contact with G.P.s: 50 per cent of H.V.s had weekly or more frequent contact; 63 per cent of H.V.s considered contact satisfactory, 37 per cent unsatisfactory.

Sessional activities: 42·2 per cent of sessions spent on child health, 21 per cent on sessions in schools, 10·3 per cent on health education.

Work in child health clinics: see Chapter 6.

Work in schools: see Chapter 7.

Clerical work: 55 per cent of H.V.s had some clerical help, 28 per cent used dictaphones.

Clear differences between work of full-time H.V.s and triple-duty H.V.s, particularly in respect of social problems, G.P. referrals, and involvement in group health education.

Researchers' Conclusions: "The traditional emphasis of the health visitor on maternal and child care has widened to include care and advice to the whole family. . . . There should be increased delegation of duties not requiring the health visitor's skills to others in the community nursing team. We wonder whether the selection and training of health visitors is keeping pace with the change in medical practice and the needs in the field".

STUDY NO. 4*

Name of Researchers: Ambler, M., Anderson, J. A. D., Black, M., Draper, P., Lewis, J., Moss, W., and Murrell, T. G. C.

Type of Project: Independent study, financed by the Nuffield Provincial Hospitals Trust, carried out by the Social Medicine Unit, Guys Hospital.

Publication:

(a) Ambler, M. *et al* (1968). The Attachment of Local Health Authority Staff to General Practices. *Medical Officer* No. 3123, Vol. CXIX, No. 22, pp. 295–299.

(b) *Health Visitor,* **41,** 9, 421–425.

Date of Study: 1967.

Location: 3 unidentified towns (county boroughs).

Aims/Purpose of Study: To examine some of the arguments for and against attachment and concentrate on the part of the health visitor's work related to attachment.

Sample:
Town A (attached): 22 health visitors
Town D1 (some liaison): 16 health visitors
Town D2 (traditional): 13 health visitors
Three separate work studies in each area lasted one week each.

Method: Three different work records were completed by the health visitors in all three towns giving the following information:
(a) time spent on different duties.
(b) communications with different agencies about clients.
(c) the content of home visits and interviews with clients.
All the health visitors were interviewed by a member of the research team using a structured schedule. Most of the G.P.s were also interviewed.

Main Findings:
Allocation of time: see Table 2 and 4.
Clientele: "In all three towns traditional work with mothers and young children accounted for the majority of the health visitors' time".
Contact with G.P.s was much greater in Town A (attached), health visitors spent more time in contact with G.P.s and communicated with more families. Only two out of 51 health visitors had access to G.P.s records.
Views of G.P.s and H.V.s about attachment not included in this review.

Researchers' Conclusions: "While it has been possible to show that the patterns of work were different, it is much more difficult to demonstrate that any differences have been caused by attachment. . . . Our findings suggest that the advantages of health visitors' attachments outweigh the disadvantages".

STUDY NO. 5

Name of Researcher: Atkinson, M. G.
Type of Project: Management survey (Chief Nursing Officer for County Council).
Publication: Survey Into the Work of the Health Visitor. Health in the West Riding, 1971, pp. 13–19.
Date of Study: 1970 (Mid-April–June).
Location: West Riding of Yorkshire.
Aims/Purpose of Study: To review the overall volume of work; to detect any new trends arising from working in general practice situations and to see what work could be delegated by health visitors to assistants and others.
Sample: All health visitors and assistants to health visitors in post; 264 health visitors. Work was recorded for two weeks.
Method: Respondents completed a schedule of all their work activities for a period of two weeks. Work time was coded according to activity and results tabulated as percentages of total time. A three-day pilot survey checked the code sheet.
Main Findings:
Allocation of time: see Table 2.
Percentages of time spent on various types of visits (24 per cent), i.e. types of clinic work (17·4 per cent), types of school work (9·1 per cent) and clerical work (25·1 per cent) are separately tabulated.

The overall volume of work showed a high proportion of time spent on clerical work, and insufficient time on effective home visiting, in spite of the valuable support from SRN Assistants to Health Visitors.

No new trends were demonstrated arising from G.P. attachment situations.

Researcher's Conclusions: This was a worthwhile piece of work, stimulating health visitors to consider for themselves how they could use clerical help, e.g. rationalising filing systems to some degree. It demonstrated to the county as a whole the range of work done by a health visitor, leading to wider use of SRN staff in some divisions, and encouraged the SRN by listing all their work and suggesting the need for regular in-service help.

STUDY NO. 6*

Name of Researcher: Carter, F.

Type of Project: M.Sc. Dissertation (Dept. of Engineering Production, University of Birmingham).

Publication: Carter, F. (1973). The Activities of General Practice. M.Sc. dissertation. University of Birmingham. Unpublished.

(Note: This work formed part of a study commissioned by the Office of Health Economics and is incorporated in Appendix 1 of O.H.E. (1974) The Work of Primary Medical Care.)

Date of Study: 1972 (August).

Location: National sample.

Aims/Purpose of Study: To describe the pattern of work of the medical and administrative work of general practice.

Sample: A random sample of 10 per cent of G.P.s in the U.K. was contacted. Fifty-eight practices completed a survey of the work of the doctor, nurse, health visitor and secretary; the respondents included 20 health visitors (18 full-time, two part-time).

Participants recorded their work for one week.

Method: A postal survey was designed using systematic activity sampling. The activity sampling sheet was designed to cater for all members of general practice staff, thus the categories of activity (eight) had been fairly broad. A "job profile" was used to obtain details of the job and respondents were asked to rank their activities according to the amount of time they took and to indicate the degree of job satisfaction given by each. In addition a "practice profile" obtained details about the practice such as list size and details of staff.

Main Findings: Allocation of time: see Table 2.

(Other findings concerned other types of staff.)

Researcher's Conclusions: Not given.

STUDY NO. 7*

Name of Researcher: City of Leicester, Town Clerk's Dept., Management Services Branch.

Type of Project: O & M project commissioned by employing authority.

Publication: Unpublished (confidential) report.

Date of Study: October 1968–May 1969.

Location: Leicester (city).

Aims/Purposes of Study: The three-phase project was designed to establish a mathematical formula based on standards of nursing required by the M.O.H.

which would be used to translate caseloads into exact health visiting requirements. The specific aims of Phase 1 (analysis of health visitor work content) were:

(1) to provide vital statistical information such as the mean duration of home visits, the proportion of time spent on health visiting activities, and various other details of work content which would then be utilised to determine coefficients in the staffing formula;

(2) to examine in detail the recording and clerical duties performed by health visitors with a view to providing additional clerical assistance, thereby enabling health visitors to devote more time to effective visiting duties.

Sample: All full-time health visitors in post (29 health visitors); the exclusion of six part-time health visitors and data loss due to sickness, etc. reduced the sample to 70 per cent of the total health visiting staff. For the secondary detailed survey of clerical tasks the sample was reduced to 58 per cent. Work was recorded for four weeks.

Method: Health visitors used pocket-sized tape recorders to record their start and finish time for each activity and a brief description of the activity. The survey was staggered because of the limited number of machines available, but each health visitor recorded activities for four weeks. The tape recordings were transcribed and analysed to determine for each health visitor:

(a) the percentage of effective working time spent on each health visiting activity;

(b) the total time per week on each health visiting activity;

(c) the average number of times each activity is performed per month;

(d) the average duration of each activity.

A secondary survey of clerical work was undertaken in which health visitors were asked to record the exact time spent performing individual clerical tasks for a period of two weeks by means of self-recording sheets.

Main Findings:

Allocation of time: see Table 2 and 3.

The mean duration of home visits to young children was 22 minutes, and to elderly persons 28 minutes; the mean duration of "unscheduled street stops" was nine minutes.

The mean number of effective home visits was 116 per month and of ineffective home visits was 24 per month. The mean number of "collective visits" (i.e. clinic and other sessions) was 21 per month.

Researchers' Conclusions: "The most outstanding feature in the results of the survey is the excessively high proportion of time spent by health visitors performing clerical duties. It is clear from the clerical breakdown that most of this time is devoted to the updating, transferring and filing of medical records. Following detailed investigation into the content of each of the clerical duties it became apparent that a large proportion of the clerical work undertaken by health visitors could be performed by a clerk/audio typist".

STUDY NO. 8

Name of Researcher: Clark, M. J.
Type of Project: Thesis M.Phil., University of Reading 1972.
Publication:
(a) A Family Visitor: A Descriptive Analysis of Health Visiting in Berkshire. London. Royal College of Nursing. 1973.

(b) What Do Health Visitors Do?: *Nursing Times* (Occasional Papers), 1972, **68,** 30, 117–119.

(c) The "New Breed" Health Visitor: *Nursing Times* (Occasional Papers), 1972, **68,** 31, 121–122.

(d) The Effect of Attachment on the Work of the Health Visitor: *Nursing Times* (Occasional Papers), 1972, **68,** 31, 123–124.

(e) The Role of the Health Visitor: A Study Conducted in Berkshire, England. Journal of Advanced Nursing, 1976, 1, 25–36.

Date of Study: May–July, 1969.

Location: Berkshire.

Aims/Purpose of Study:

(1) To describe the work of the health visitor in terms which would show the range of subject matter concerned within the statutory duties described as "maternal and child welfare".

To examine the extent to which the H.V. was extending her work to groups other than mothers with young children.

To explore the anxieties expressed by health visitors about their role and their relationships with other workers.

Sample: All general health visitors in Berkshire on 1 May 1969 (82 health visitors). Response rate 87·8 per cent. Data based on 2,057 visits recorded by 72 health visitors. Visits were recorded for one week.

Method: Respondents completed a specially designed "visit schedule" for every visit made during their "study week". The study also included an interview with the health visitors about their work and a questionnaire about contacts with selected social agencies.

Main Findings: (Findings related to the study of home visits only, other findings are not included here.)

Clientele: 71 per cent of visits were to families with young children, 18 per cent to the elderly, 11 per cent to other households.

Source of Visit: The H.V. initiated 63·5 per cent of visits, the client 13·6 per cent, the G.P. 7·3 per cent.

Purpose: The most common purpose was a routine visit to a young child, but this comprised only a quarter of the total; 80 per cent of visits were planned.

Length: Most visits (79 per cent) lasted less than half an hour; 28 per cent lasted less than 15 minutes, but 3·4 per cent lasted longer than an hour.

Content: All 52 topics listed were mentioned. The most frequently recorded topic was infant feeding, which was recorded in 37 per cent of visits. Topics not specifically concerned with young children were recorded in more than 80 per cent of visits. The proportion of topics concerned with social and emotional aspects was significantly greater in visits to families where there were no young children, and in those initiated by the G.P.

In 60 per cent of the visits the H.V. was thought to be the only visitor.

There were significant differences, most marked in the content of visits and the approach of the H.V., between H.V.s of different age groups and different dates of training.

Researcher's Conclusions:

The work of the health visitor is far more varied than the stereotype.

The role of "family visitor" cannot be developed to its full potential without an increase in the number of health visitors; health visitors must determine their priorities.

There is no evidence that attachment to general practice results in direction by the G.P. of the health visitor's work or in a move towards curative work. If changes in the training of H.V.s are not reflected in changes in the service, there is a danger that newly qualified H.V.s are training for a job which they are not allowed to do.

STUDY NO. 9*

Name of Researcher: Clow, J. T.
Type of Project: Dissertation for the Diploma of Public Health, University of Leeds.
Publication: "Attachment of Health Visitors to General Practitioners": *Nursing Times* (Occasional Papers), 18 October 1968.
Date of Study: 1966 (November).
Location: West Riding of Yorkshire.
Aims/Purpose of Study: To assess the results of the change of work patterns caused by the introduction of attachment schemes.
Sample: 48 health visitors from six separate divisions, 24 attached and 24 non-attached; method of selection of sample not specified.
Work was recorded for one week (substitute days allowed where necessary).
Method: Participants timed and recorded their work, using a coded proforma diary sheet, for one week. Pilot study involving nine health visitors lasted one week. Two "practice days" were used to accustom participants to the method. Activities were divided into seven groups: visits to expectant mothers and under fives; visits to persons aged over 65 years; miscellaneous visits; attendance at clinics; school health work; formal health education; miscellaneous activities.
Main Findings:
Allocation of time: see Table 2.
Clientele: 56 per cent of visits were to expectant mothers and under fives, 23 per cent to elderly persons, 20 per cent to others.
11·5 per cent of visits were "ineffective" (i.e. no reply)
The main differences between attached and non-attached health visitors were that the attached health visitor spends less time in visiting, more in clinic work (including surgery work), more on consultation, slightly less on travelling.
Researcher's Conclusions: "Two salient facts emerge. First, the change-over to attachment has not resulted in any disruption of the service and, secondly, there is a satisfactory increase in the personal contact between the health visitor and the G.P. Such differences as are apparent are only marginal".

STUDY NO. 10*

Name of Researcher: Dawtrey, E.
Type of Project: M.Phil. thesis. C.N.A.A. Polytechnic of North London (Medical Architecture Research Unit) 1977.
Publication: Unpublished.
Date of Study: 1975.
Location: London.
Aims/Purpose of Study: "To look at the work of the health visitor in the health centre with particular emphasis on two contrasting ways of organising her work" (i.e. attached/non-attached).

Sample: Random one in five sample of the case records of two health visitors (one attached, one non-attached) in one health centre; case-load defined as those cases seen in previous 12 months; sample size (total) 112 (attached health visitors 58; non-attached 54).

Method: One in five sample of case-notes, taking the data from the last visit made to a patient within previous 12 months. Each "data item" was recorded on index card, categorised as follows:

(1) Reason for origin of contact:
    (a) new birth
    (b) elderly
    (c) other
(2) Last contact:
    (d) home visit
    (e) health centre
    (f) other
(3) Reason for last contact:
    (g) health advice
    (h) family planning
    (i) ante-natal or post-natal
    (j) family problems or support
(4) Referred to:
    (k) health centre
    (l) G.P./hospital
    (m) local authority
    (n) other
    (o) none
(5) Comments

Main Findings: Statistically significant differences were found between the two health visitors in:

(1) origin of contact (i.e. type of case);
(2) reason for last contact (i.e. content).

Researcher's Conclusions: For discussion of health visiting records, see page 88.

STUDY NO. 11

Name of Researchers: Ellwood, M. and Jeffereys, M.

Type of Project: Part of a study of the development of a new health centre, undertaken by the Social Research Unit, Bedford College (University of London), commissioned by D.H.S.S. (see also Study No. 24).

Publication: Unpublished work summarised and reviewed by Hicks, D. (1976), Primary Medical Care. H.M.S.O. pp. 285–288.

Date of Study: November 1971–October 1972. This forms part of the data collected before the move into the new health centre.

Location: London.

Aims/Purpose of Study: To record the activities of two groups of general practitioners and practice-based staff, and the health-related behaviour and attitudes of their patients before, during, and after their move into a new health centre.

Sample: 11 health visitors (one part-time) working in four units of which two were general practice units and two were Family Health Clinics. The health visitor recorded their work for a period of a year.

Method: A new "weekly return" form was developed jointly by the participant health visitors, management and the research team. The forms were completed for a year. Data were coded and tabulated to provide information for the sample of health visitors as a whole and for each team or unit on:

(a) age distribution of cases seen
(b) place of contact
(c) reasons for contact
(d) referrals
(e) time spent by health visitors on various activities.

Main Findings:

Allocation of time: see Table 2.

The findings were compared with those of Clark (Study No. 8) and showed a wider range of clients with more varied problems.

Inter-unit or team comparisons revealed differences between units which were interpreted as due to "many factors" including "differences in the outlooks and policies of the units in which the health visitors were based, differences in the kinds of referrals that were made to them and differences in facilities available to them to provide services for their clients".

Researchers' Conclusions: Not given in Hicks' review.

STUDY NO. 12*

Name of Researchers: Fry, J., Dillane, J. B. and Conolly, M.

Type of Project: Report by one practice team of their own work.

Publication: "The Evolution of a Health Team: A Successful General Practitioner-Health Visitor Association". *British Medical Journal*, 1965, 1, 181–183.

Date of Study: June 1963–May 1964.

Location: London.

Aims/Purpose of Study:

(a) "to describe the effects of an attachment of a health visitor to a London suburban practice";

(b) "to enumerate for others the necessary steps for success".

Sample: One health visitor kept records of her work for one year.

Method: Health visitor kept her own (routine?) records of her work for a year.

Main Findings:

Three quarters of the visits were routine visits to children, and 12 per cent to elderly persons.

Approximately the same number of clients were seen in the surgery as were seen in home visits.

Researchers' Conclusions: "We believe that this concept of G.P.-H.V. attachment will spread so quickly that within 10 years it will be accepted as the normal pattern of work for both doctor and health visitor".

STUDY NO. 13*

Name of Researchers: Gallaher, E., Howe, J. E., McNeil, A. W. and Richardson, E. M.

Type of Subject: O & M study commissioned by employing authority.

Publication: "A Study of Health Visiting and District Nursing in Bolton". *Medical Officer*—27 March 1970, pp. 161–167.

Date of Study: 1966 (February).

Location: Bolton.

Aims/Purpose of Study: To find out:

(a) how much of any of the work of the health visitor and district nurses can be carried out by staff having a lesser qualification.

(b) what means there are of enabling health visitors and district nurses to spend a greater protion of their time with clients.

Sample: All health visitors in the Borough of Bolton; 40 health visitors (including nine part-time staff). Work recorded continuously "until fluctuation in the percentage for each activity levelled off and the same percentage began to recur daily". (Four weeks.)

Method: Health visitors completed a "daily activity report" designed by the O & M Department, recording "start" and "stop" times for each activity throughout the day. The forms were collected daily by the Superintendent Nursing Officers who scrutinised them before passing them to the Work Study/O & M Department for processing. The findings were used to calculate performance targets.

Main Findings:

Allocation of time: see Table 2.

Of the 799 hours "at visit", only 17 hours could, in the opinion of the health visitors, have been carried out by some other type of worker.

After the introduction of the performance targets, the amount of visiting increased by 38 per cent.

Researchers' Conclusions: A number of changes in administrative arrangements were recommended and performance targets were introduced.

STUDY NO. 14*

Name of Researcher: Gettings, B.

Type of Project: Management project (undertaken by County Nursing Officer).

Publication: "Health Visiting Needs in General Practice", *Health Visitor,* 1970, **43,** 43–45.

Date of Study: November 1967–October 1968.

Location: Berkshire.

Aims/Purpose of Study: "For internal use only, as a guide to current developments and changing trends.

(1) To ascertain whether or not all health visiting needs were being met.

(2) To test the value of using different categories for statistics (with a view to changing format of routine returns).

(3) To determine a realistic workload".

Sample: One health visitor (2/5 whole-time equivalent) supernumerary to existing staff, for one year.

Method: An additional health visitor was appointed supernumerary to an existing primary health care team consisting of seven G.P.s, 1·5 health visitors, 1·0 district nurse, 0·5 midwife (7,400 patients). She accepted referrals from the rest of the team, being introduced to clients as "the special health visitor". Originally one half day per week was allocated, but this rapidly grew to two days to meet demand. The special health visitor kept detailed notes of her work for one year, using a specially designed case record.

Main Findings: The special health visitor made 457 visits to 70 families, in $65\frac{1}{2}$ days.

64 families referred by G.P.s, six by nursing team.

Two families (3 per cent) referred to social worker for intensive casework.

Clientele included all social classes and all age groups.

Researcher's Conclusions: Number of visits and time required was extrapolated to estimate "ideal" health visiting caseloads.

All health visiting needs are not being met at present.

The use of problem categories for returns of work done shows what the health visitor's work involves. If used extensively it would be a valuable guide to changing trends nationally.

A realistic workload for a health visitor is an average of 1,610 visits per year or equivalent sessions.

A ratio of one health visitor to 3,700 population is indicated.

Health visiting in general practice is family health visiting and covers the full range of health visiting duties.

Reported satisfaction of clients, doctors, and health visitors, "standard of health visitor practice raised".

STUDY NO. 15*

Name of Researcher: Gettings, B.

Type of Project: Management survey (undertaken by County Nursing Officer).

Publication: "A School Nursing Work Study in Berkshire". *Health Visitor,* 1971, **44,** 9, 285–288.

Date of Study: 1969 (February).

Location: Berkshire.

Aims/Purpose of Study: Not Specified.

Sample: All nursing staff involved in work in schools, i.e. health visitors, school nurses, school nursing auxiliaries. Numbers not given.

Method: Participants completed a specially designed diary sheet, recording the start and finish times of each activity and coding each activity by type, type of person attended to, topic and technique or action. The total number of hours recorded (i.e. all health visitors together) were analysed.

Main Findings: (N.B. Only findings related to health visitors included in this review.)

The distribution of total time (hours and percentage reported) was 57·8 per cent on health teaching 17·8 per cent on liason with school staff, 7·1 per cent on youth counselling, 5·8 per cent on other duties (mainly home visiting), and 11·3 per cent on travelling associated with these duties.

Researcher's Conclusions: "The total amount of health visiting time spent on school health is low; this is in accordance with the policy of giving school nurses the responsibility for their nursing duties. While there may be a need to aim at a marginal increase in health education, youth counselling and liason, the results on the whole are satisfactory."

STUDY NO. 16*

Name of Researcher: Gilmore, M.

Type of Project: Pilot study for larger study (No. 17) commissioned by the C.E.T.H.V., funded by the (then) Ministry of Health.

Publication: "A Pilot Study of the Work of a Nursing Team in General Practice". *Medical Officer* 1970, **124,** 18, 238–243.

107

Date of Study: November 1967–October 1968.

Location: Brighton.

Aims/Purpose of Study: "The overall aim of the study was an assessment of the work of the nursing team; in particular it was concerned with the type and range of work done by each nurse, the extent of medical nursing and social needs of the families in the practice population as ascertained by the health visitors and the type of problems referred by the nurses to social and medical services".

Sample: One primary health care team, including two health visitors, one of whom was designated team leader. (Two G.P.s, population 7,689).

The study period lasted one year; work record forms were completed for a period of two weeks, visits were recorded for one year.

Method: A specially recruited nursing team was attached to a general practice, following a one-week induction course. Additional counselling was given on a series of visits to the team at intervals throughout the study year. The data for the study were collected by means of record forms completed by the nurses on each home visit, by records of clinics and health education classes held, by records of time spent by each nurse on various activities over a period of two weeks.

Main Findings:

Allocation of time: see Table 2.

The health visitor visited 26 per cent of the practice population; half of the visits were to children under five, and 16 per cent to single persons living alone.

43 per cent of visits were initiated by the G.P., and of these, half were to elderly patients and about one eighth to families with young children; 72 per cent of all first visits were to families in which there was illness or disability.

In their 1,633 visits, the health visitors found 211 untreated medical needs (154 patients) and 734 social needs (62 per cent of families).

Researcher's Conclusions:

"It is likely that the most significant change in the work of the health visitors was in the high proportion of visits made to families with illness in home".

"Shift in emphasis from families with young children to the elderly and other age groups due in part to G.P. referrals ... and to visits to those receiving district nursing care".

Machinery is required to maximise the case-finding potential of working in attachment.

System of communication between hospital and community team is needed for care of patients discharged from hospital.

"Large number of social needs noted and dealt with by health visitors ... raises the necessity for a clear definition of her role vis a vis that of the social worker."

"The marked fall in the number of home visits and the amount of time spent on office work was a disturbing feature of this study".

Need for someone to co-ordinate team, "not necessarily for 'leader' in sense of one member exercising authority over the others".

Need for training of team members in:

(a) development of case-finding skills.

(b) relationship of health visitors and district nurses to other members of nurse team and full use of ancillary staff.

(c) team work: the study of group dynamics.

Name of Researchers: Gilmore, M., Bruce, N. and Hunt, M.
Type of Project: Large scale project commissioned by C.E.T.H.V. and funded by D.H.S.S.
M.Phil. thesis. (M. Hunt).

Publication:
(a) "The Work of the Nursing Team in General Practice". London. C.E.T.H.V. 1974.
(b) (M. Hunt). "Factors Influencing Teamwork in General Medical Practice". M.Phil. thesis, University of Edinburgh. Unpublished.

Date of Study: 1972–1973.
Location: Main study Scotland, extended study England.
Aims/Purpose of Study: "to obtain information that would provide some basis for the assessment of the training needs of health visitors working in general practice teams. . . . To obtain such information the study was focused on exploring the ways in which the resources of general practice could be utilised by health visitors in developing the services they provided and on identification of the factors that fostered and hindered this development".

In addition to the main study, an "extension study" of 36 other teams was carried out with the following aims:
(1) To find out the composition of the teams and the sizes of the practice populations they served.
(2) To discover what methods the team used to communicate with each other.
(3) To find out the range of clinics and group activities carried out by the teams.
(4) To identify the perceptions the G.P.s, health visitors and district nurses held regarding their own and each others professional activities and responsibilities and the extent to which discrepancies in perceptions were displayed.
(5) To assess the extent to which discrepancies existed between the expectations team members held in relation to what they considered should be the division of professional work and responsibilities between them and what they perceived actually happened in practice.
(6) To discover to what extent team members revealed awareness of ambiguities and conflicts in team relationships and what mechanisms were utilised to deal with any conflicts which existed.

Sample:
(a) *main study:* three teams selected on the basis of presence of 10 criteria concerning size, structure and practice organisation. Only one team could be found which met all criteria; the other two met seven of the 10.
(b) *extended study:* teams selected on less rigorous criteria (3) yielded population of 82 teams in England and Scotland; 50 per cent random sample taken excluding "special cases"—yielded 36 teams comprising 174 G.P.s, 70 health visitors, and 57 district nurses. Response rates: G.P.s 79 per cent, health visitors 88 per cent, district nurses 85 per cent.
The study lasted one year.

Methods:
(a) Main Study:
Three teams were established, one with an induction course and subsequent counselling service and a team co-ordinator. Meetings and counselling sessions were recorded and observed throughout the study year.

109

For two separate periods of two weeks the health visitors and district nurses kept a timed record of their working days' activities.

For two periods, one of one month and one of two months, the health visitors and district nurses completed record forms of all home visits.

Research secretary in each centre recorded number and type of clinics and attendance at them.

Questionnaires and interviews with all staff.

Observation of team meetings in two of the centres.

(b) Extension Study:

Each team was visited by the researcher, who interviewed team members, and left questionnaires to be self-administered by respondents and returned by post.

Main Findings: (N.B. The major findings relate to the dynamics of teamwork; only the findings related to the work of the health visitor are included in this review.)

Allocation of time: see Table 2.

Few "teams" had any systematic preparation for engaging in teamwork, or any systematic system for communication or decision making.

Minimal use was made of age-sex registers even in the three "main" study teams where registers were provided. One in seven of the health visitors visits in two centres and one in three in the third centre was initiated by G.P.s.

In two centres more than half the home visits paid by health visitors were to children under five; in the third centre the proportion was one third, and half of the visits were to the elderly.

60 per cent of the visits in two centres and 46 per cent in the third centre were made for the reason of "age only".

The most common activity in home visits was "health counselling".

All the health visitors identified unmet medical needs and social needs; in general more social needs were identified by health visitors than by district nurses.

The health visitors made more contacts with outside agencies than the district nurses; the majority of contacts were with social service departments.

Researchers' Conclusions:

Participants believed in the benefits of teamwork.

Achievement of teamwork is not automatic but requires deliberate action.

The potential of attachment is not being fully utilised.

The role of the co-ordinator showed promise and required further study.

STUDY NO. 18*

Name of Researcher: Graham, J. A. G.

Type of Project: Work study project undertaken by employing authority.

Publication: "A Health Visitor Work Study". *Medical Officer* 1966, 116, 27.

Date of Study: 1965 (1 January–30 April).

Location: Worthing.

Aims/Purpose of Study: To analyse the health visitor's work, comparing non-attached health visitors work with that of attached health visitors—before embarking on further attachments.

Sample: Six non-attached health visitors.

Two attached health visitors (in post four months at 1 January, 1965).

Method: Detailed records of work done were kept by the health visitors. Methodology not explained in any detail.

Main Findings:

Distribution of time: see Table 2.

The number of visits per day ranged from 6·6 to 12·6.

The attached health visitors recorded a lower proportion of visits to children and a higher proportion of visits to the elderly than the non-attached health visitors.

Researcher's Conclusions: Not Specified.

STUDY NO. 19

Name of Researcher: Henderson, Jill C.

Type of Project: M.Sc. Dissertation, (University of Surrey).

Publication:

(a) "Health Visiting in Hampshire". M.Sc. Dissertation. University of Surrey, 1977. Unpublished.

(b) "What Do Health Visitors Do?" *Nursing Mirror,* 14 September 1978, pp. 30–32.

Date of Study: October, 1975.

Location: Hampshire.

Aims/Purpose of Study: To describe the day to day work of the health visitor in Hampshire A.H.A. with particular reference to the clientele served on home visits.

Sample: All general health visitors in Hampshire who were working for any part of the survey period (212 health visitors). Response rate 86 per cent. Data obtained from 183 health visitors, recorded over a period of two weeks.

Method: Respondents completed a precoded diary sheet of all their activities for two weeks; they also completed a personal questionnaire.

Main Findings:

The highest percentage of time was spent on domiciliary visiting (23 per cent).

Second to this came administration (21 per cent).

The greatest number of domiciliary visits were concerned with general child management (31 per cent).

The greatest number of visits made were to children under five (58 per cent).

There were substantial differences in work patterns related to different staffing levels in the four health districts.

64 per cent of clients visited had not been in contact with visitors from any other health or social agency within the past month.

Researcher's Conclusions:

In view of the fact that the health visitors spend more time in ancillary activities (57 per cent) than actually serving members of the public by direct face to face contact (43 per cent), the extent to which some duties can be delegated to others needs further consideration.

In view of the relationship between staffing levels and work patterns, greater precision is needed in determining priorities in health visiting on a national basis.

Name of Researcher: Jefferys, M.

Type of Project: Independent study undertaken on the initiative of Buckinghamshire County Council, by the Dept. of Public Health at the London School of Hygiene and Tropical Medicine, funded by the Nuffield Provincial Hospitals Trust.

Publication: "An Anatomy of Social Welfare Services". London. Michael Joseph. 1965.

Date of Study: 1960–61.

Location: Buckinghamshire.

Aims/Purpose of Study: "an attempt to obtain for the first time a representative picture of the whole field of social services at work in one county.... It was designed to examine simultaneously and systematically the work of staff in different branches of the social services, and the characteristics of those served".

Sample: The survey covered the work of:

district nurse/midwives

health visitors

medical social workers

welfare and mental welfare officers

home help organisers

home teachers of the blind, social workers in child guidance clinics, special welfare workers, school attendance officers, youth employment officers, youth leaders, child care officers, policewomen, probation officers, G.P.s, voluntary organisations.

Health visitors: population of 47 full time health visitors, one part time health visitor, 16 "triple duty workers".

Response: 46 health visitors for some parts, 42 for others.

Method: Staff completed a record sheet for every individual seen during a specific week in the twelve month study period (October 1960–September 1961) or for a consecutive sequence of 25 cases if fewer than 25 were seen during the week, plus summary diary sheet.

Staff were interviewed about their personal characteristics, training, views about their work, etc.

Main Findings: (N.B. Chapter 4 of the book is entitled "The Health Visiting Service").

Distribution of time: see Table 2.

In 87 per cent of households visited there was at least one pre-school child; one in 20 visits were to elderly people.

The health visitors, unlike most other social welfare staff, visited a fairly representative social cross-section.

Health visitors identified social problems in one third of families visited, and chronic physical disability, mental illness, or sub-normality in one fifth.

Researcher's Conclusions: Considerable discussion of health visitors' possible future role, analysis of their low morale and uncertainty about status, etc.

Name of Researcher: Loveland, M.

Type of Project: Thesis (M.Phil), University of Surrey.

Publication:
(a) The Work of Health Visitors in an Urban and County Area In Relation to Health Visitor Training in the University of Surrey. M.Phil thesis. University of Surrey 1970.
(b) The Work of Health Visitors in an Urban and County Area In Relation to Health Visitor Training in the University of Surrey. *Nursing Times* (Occasional Papers) 3 June 1971, pp. 85–87.

Date of Study: 1968.
Location: Merton (London) and Wiltshire.
Aims/Purpose of Study: To discover if training fitted the health visitor for the work she was doing.
Sample: All health visitors in both areas: 27 in Merton, 64 in Wiltshire.
Response rate: 100 per cent in Merton, 80 per cent in Wiltshire.
Data obtained from 91 health visitors, for 20 consecutive working days. An additional survey of three days work of 20 health visitors in each area was undertaken.
Method: A questionnaire was completed by each health visitor for each day. A personal record form was also distributed by the superintendent. Analysis of this information suggested that further information was required, and so an additional survey was undertaken. Each health visitor was also asked to write a diary of the day's work on one specified date. (16 May 1968).
Main Findings:
The health visitors spent on average 74 minutes per day on clerical work; (time on other activities not specified in the report).
Between 54 per cent and 62 per cent of the visits were to children between the ages of one and five years.
In the 20 days surveyed health visitors made contact with 61 different categories of other workers.
Researcher's Conclusions: "As a result of these surveys it can be assumed that the training at the University of Surrey adequately prepares the health visitor for the work she is at present expected to do in the county and urban areas, but with the changing pattern of health visiting other skills may need to be developed".

STUDY NO. 22*

Name of Researcher: Marris, T.
Type of Project: Survey undertaken by the Itelligence Unit of the G.L.C. at the request of the C.E.T.H.V. and the Association of London Borough Medical Officers of Health.
Publication: "The Work of Health Visitors in London". G.L.C. Department of Planning and Transportation. Research Report No. 12. 1971.
Date of Study: October 1969.
Location: Greater London.
Aims/Purpose of Study: "To examine exactly what it is the London health visitors are engaged on in their day to day activities".
Sample: One in five sample, taken from an alphabetical list of all health visitors working in the 32 boroughs of the G.L.C. area. Final sample size 215 health

visitors. Work recorded for two weeks. Analysis of 2,015 whole health visiting days, 49 part days, 18 part weekends.

Method: Diary sheets were sent to respondents two weeks before the survey period. Briefing meetings (8) held during week prior to survey. Diary sheets were completed for two weeks and then returned to researcher by post. The diary sheet was completed from a code book, recording start and finishing times for each activity, nature of activity (24 coded), person served (37 codes), topics (38 codes), technique and action (15 codes).

Personal details about respondents were collected by separate questionnaire.

Main Findings: Results were grouped to compare Inner, Middle and Outer Boroughs, and length of experience of health visitor. Distribution of total time (1,050, 864 minutes) between the various activities, people served, place of work, topics and techniques, is presented as a percentage of total recorded time and minutes per activity/person served/topic.

Distribution of time: see Table 2.

The health visitors' clientele: see Table 8 and Table 14.

Topics recorded and time spent on each topic: see Table 22.

Researcher's Conclusions: The range of content of work was shown to be very wide.

STUDY NO. 23*

Name of Researcher: Ministry of Health.

Type of Project: Research undertaken for and published in government report.

Publication: An Enquiry Into Health Visiting: Report of the Working Party on the field of work, training, and recruitment of health visitors (Jameson Report). H.M.S.O. 1956.

Date of Study: 1955.

Location: Six areas: Newcastle, Northumberland, Glasgow, Ayrshire, Cardiff, Glamorgan.

Aims/Purpose of Study: To provide data supplementary to the evidence presented to the committee by interested groups, to help the committee to formulate its recommendations.

Sample:

(a) Newcastle and Northumberland: one in five sample of staff available during selected study week—Newcastle 12, Northumberland 11.

(b) Glasgow: One in five of maternity and child welfare visitors (20), T.B. visitors (8), and housing inspectresses (5), with one in ten of school nurses (4). (Total 37.)

(c) Ayrshire: All 10 qualified health visitors plus one in six of the rest (10). (Total 20.)

(d) Glamorgan: 14 health visitors selected from alphabetical lists in each of eight divisional areas.

(e) Cardiff: 10 out of 24 general duty health visitors plus six specialist health visitors.

Overall total: 77 generalist health visitors, 23 specialist health visitors.

Diaries kept for one week.

Method: The health visitors were given instructions how to keep the diaries "shortly before the selected week", allowed one practice day, and asked to record all work for one week. The week varied from one area to another, chosen to avoid, for example, holiday periods. The weeks were spread over a period of four months. Diary sheets recorded time, object of visit, brief note on case, problems posed, additional problems, action taken.

Diary sheet reproduced as Appendix VIIc of report.

Main Findings: Distribution of time: see Table 2.

Researchers' Conclusions: "in the ordinary course of her work and without exceeding her competence, she (the health visitor) could be in a real sense a general purpose family visitor".

STUDY NO. 24*

Name of Researcher: Morris, M. E.

Type of Project: Management project undertaken by nurse managers.

Publication: Unpublished report Preston Health District, Lancashire Area Health Authority.

Date of Study:

(a) November–December 1975.

(b) Clerical activity survey June–July 1976.

Location: Preston, Lancashire.

Aims/Purpose of Study: "For health visitors to look in depth at their own work to see if any redeployment is necessary".

Sample: All health visitors in Preston health districts. 62 health visitors, 20 working days (four weeks).

Method: Diary sheets completed for 20 consecutive working days (four weeks).

(a) Daily diary sheet, work recorded in units of 15 minutes; opinions about possible delegation were recorded.

(b) Weekly diary sheet, time spent (in minutes) on various activities.

Main Findings:

(1) Distribution of time: see Table 2.

(2) Activities in schools: see Table 16.

(3) Clerical work: see Table 19.

Researcher's Conclusions: Not Given.

STUDY NO. 25*

Name of Researcher: Naidoo, J.

Type of Project: Part of a study of the development of a new health centre, undertaken by the Social Research Unit, Bedford Colege (University of London), commissioned by the D.H.S.S. (see also Study No. 11).

Publication: "A Preliminary Analysis of the Visiting Patterns of Attached and Non-attached Health Visitors'. Unpublished paper. Social Research Unit, Bedford College, University of London. 1977.

Date of Study: Summer, 1976.

Location: London (Kentish Town).

Aims/Purpose of Study: "To consider two questions:

(1) Are there significant differences in the work of attached and non-attached health visitors?

(2) If there are, can they be explained by differences in the population being visited or is there some other factor, to do with attachement as such, which is responsible for the differences?"

115

Sample: 11 health visitors (eight full time, three part time) in four teams in the same locality.

Team A—Two full time, one part time, attached, in a health centre (no schedules received from the part time worker, due to ill-health).

Team B —Two full time, two part time, attached, in a health centre.

Team C—Three full time, not attached, in a health centre.

Team D—One full time, attached, not in a health centre.

All visits recorded for three weeks, total 463 schedules.

(N.B. under-recording noted in comparison with AHA returns).

Method: This study was part of the larger study of Health Centres. The health visitors were asked to complete a schedule for all visits for three weeks.

The schedules were coded, with 10 per cent check, punched and analysed by computer into:

(a) Breakdown of visiting patterns by attachment/non-attachment.

(b) assessment of importance of intervening variables (population characteristics) in explaining the differences.

(c) breakdown of visiting patterns by team.

Main Findings:

"Several slight differences in types of visits done and subsequent action taken by C workers, but these do not appear to be highly significant and do not add up to a holistic account of C workers operating in a different way to other workers".

"Highly significant differences between teams do exist for most of the variables looked at".

"Variance testing indicated that of all the factors looked at, "team" was the most powerful followed by marital status and dates of qualification as SRN and health visitor".

Characteristics concerning clientele being visited were eliminated as a prime source of differentiation in visiting patterns.

Researcher's Conclusions: "Team was the only factor to produce significant differences amongst all the variables looked at. This suggests that "team" alone is powerful enough to produce distinct sub-populations of health visitors and their cases. . . . Reference group theory provides a rationale for the strength of "team" over and above the other factors looked at. . . . It is suggested that "team" operates as a reference group for its members, thus manipulating attitudes and behaviour to create a "team image", a holistic approach to the functions of primary health care. . . . The hypothesis that is being advanced is that members learn to work efficiently with each other by taking the primary health care team as their reference group and adopting their ways of working to fit in with the goals and ideology of the team to which they belong."

STUDY NO. 26*

Name of Researcher: Nimmo, A. W.

Type of Project: Operational research project carried out for employing authority by the Operational Research Group, Grampian Health Services Information Unit.

Publication: "A Survey of Child Health Clinics at the Denburn Health Centre, Aberdeen". Report No. 37. Operational Research Group, Grampian Health Services Information Unit, Grampian Health Board, 1979.

Date of Study: 1978.

Location: Aberdeen.

Aims/Purpose of Study: "This pilot survey was intended to fill in a gap in knowledge about this part of health visitors' work. Few surveys of clinic sessions have been published and no attempt has previously been made to time the activities which occur at clinic sessions".

Sample: All child health clinics conducted at one health centre between 5 October 1978 and 16 November 1978. (Seven sessions). Clinic sessions were held once per week (1·45 to 4·00 pm) and were staffed by one health visitor, a health assistant, and a doctor. Number of children not given.

Method: When a mother arrived at the clinic a survey card was completed for her children, allowing details of up to three children per card. The card also recorded mode of travel to clinic, arrival time, consultation time, and the health visitor's activity (inspection, weighing, immunisation screening).

Main Findings:

Characteristics of children: almost all were 16 months or younger, most were first born children; it was rare for a mother to be accompanied by more than one child; 22 per cent were attending for the first time.

Travel: 12 per cent of mothers travelled more than a mile; 75 per cent walked, 13 per cent by car, 12 per cent came by bus.

58 per cent of all attendances were to see the health visitor only.

The average consultation time was 6·7 minutes per mother.

The "indirect" time (i.e. preparation, clerical etc.) was 105 minutes per session—almost as long as the clinic session itself.

Researcher's Conclusions: Not given.

STUDY NO. 27*

Name of Researcher: Nimmo, A. W.

Type of Project: Operational research project carried out for employing authority by the Operational Research Group, Grampian Health Services Information Unit.

Publication: "A Survey of Child Health Clinics at Seaton Clinic, Aberdeen".

Date of Study: 1979 (February–April).

Location: Aberdeen.

Aims/Purpose of Study: "To record the characteristics of children brought to the clinic, and to estimate the time spent with the health visitor at each attendance".

Sample: All child health clinic sessions at one centre between 21 February, 1979 and 4 April 1979. (Seven sessions). Sessions were held once a week, staffed by one health visitor, a health assistant, and a doctor. Number of children not given.

Method: A survey card was completed for each mother who attended, allowing details of up to three children per card. The card also recorded mode of travel, arrival time, consultation time and the health visitor's action.

Main Findings:

Characteristics of children: 88 per cent were aged 12 months or younger, and 67 per cent six months or younger; 52 per cent were first-born children; 12 per cent were attending for the first time.

60 per cent of first-born children attended to see the health visitor only, 43 per cent of subsequent children.

117

Mode of travel: 87 per cent of mothers lived within $\frac{1}{2}$ mile of the clinc and nearly all walked; 4 per cent came by car.

The average consultation time was 3·3 minutes; but 5·8 minutes for children attending for the first time.

Researcher's Conclusions: Not Given.

STUDY NO. 28

Name of Researcher: Potton, R. W.

Type of Project: Management project undertaken by S.N.O. (Research).

Publication: "Health Visitor Work Content Survey". Unpublished Report. Kent Area Health Authority. 1978.

(N.B. in addition to the main report, separate reports are available for each of the three health districts surveyed).

Date of Study: May 1977–April 1978–May 1978.

Location: Kent Area Health Authority.

Aims/Purpose of Study:

(1) To assist Management in trying to determine future resources required.

(2) To provide information on areas of support which could be supplied by other agencies at a time of recruitment difficulties.

Sample: All health visitors on duty during the survey week (134 health visitors). Data were recorded for one week in each study.

Method: Three separate surveys were undertaken in three health districts:

Tunbridge Wells Health District

Canterbury and Thanet Health District

South East Kent Health District.

The health visitors recorded all events by unit of time (in minutes) during duty hours, using a self-recording diary form which was designed in conjunction with the health visitors.

Main Findings:

A large number of tasks being performed which result in a reduction of client contact.

A need for review of clerical support.

A need to review ineffectual calls.

Clarification and greater understanding is required of the role of the Health Visitor. This has resulted in the Health Visitor being required to take upon herself tasks because a clearly defined role is not available.

Researcher's Conclusions:

It has become evident from all the studies that until the role of the Health Visitor is clearly defined to the users then possible misuse will be made of a very specialised service that is basically in short supply.

With the need to increase preventative care, it may be that greater emphasis is required in primary care. This can only really be determined by the profession itself.

STUDY NO. 29*

Name of Researcher: Poulton, K. R.

Type of Project: Management project undertaken for the District Nursing Officer by the S.N.O. (Research).

118

Publication: "Evaluation on Community Nursing Service". Unpublished Report. Wandsworth and East Merton Teaching District. 1977.

Date of Study: 1976 (September–December).

Location: London (Wandsworth and East Merton).

Aims/Purpose of Study: "To determine the operation and effectiveness of the existing community nursing services and establish differences relating to various organisational structures, i.e. attachment and alignment schemes".

Sample: (N.B. the study included district nurses and G.P.s as well as health visitors; only the health visitor's work is included in this review).

All health visitors in the health district; response rate—70 per cent. Data were obtained from 38 health visitors, who recorded their work for two weeks. (113 health visiting days).

Method: Respondents completed a specially designed diary form on which they recorded the duration, type, and location of each activity. They also completed a patient assessment form for each family visited, and a short personal questionnaire.

Main Findings:

Distribution of time: see Table 2. 30·8 per cent of time was spent on "direct clinical care".

The average duration of a visit was 24 minutes.

Most visits were made to families with small babies.

The main differences between attached and aligned health visitors were:

(a) the aligned health visitors spend more time on visits including routine visits.

(b) the attached health visitors spend more time in consultation with the G.P.

Researcher's Conclusions:

The amount of time that a health visitor spends on client contact work is low.

The communication network is extremely complex because much of the work is crisis initiated.

There is no evidence of "teamwork" among either attached or aligned health visitors.

STUDY NO. 30*

Name of Researcher: Thorpe, E. C.

Type of Project: O and M/Work Study project undertaken by the Management Services Division for the Regional Health Authority.

Publication: A report on the clerical systems related to the health visitors at the Northcote Health Clinic, Ealing.

Unpublished report. North West Thames Regional Health Authority. 1978.

Date of Study: 1978.

Location: London (Ealing).

Aims/Purpose of Study: To investigate the current clerical systems at the Northcote Health Clinic, Ealing.

Sample: Six health visitors based at one health clinic.

Method: Not specified.

Main Findings:

Health visitors estimated that they spent one quarter of their time on clerical tasks

Methods of filing and storage are not standardised and this results in difficulties when one health visitor is "covering" for another.

As health visitors have no direct control over interpreting or clerical staff, they are performing tasks which could be performed by less qualified staff.

Researcher's Conclusions: It was recommended that a new system should be introduced which transferred some of the clerical work carried out by the health visitors, to the interpreters and general clerical staff.

STUDY NO. 31

Name of Researcher: Thurmott, P. K.

Type of Project: Survey undertaken by nurse researcher for the Director of Nursing Services under the auspices of the Health Information and Research Unit, Hertfordshire County Council.

Publication: Health and the School. London. Royal College of Nursing. 1976.

Date of Study: 1973 (October).

Location: Hertfordshire.

Aims/Purpose of Study: "to assess the school nursing service in view of the enlarged role and functions which the health visitor may have", to include the following areas for investigation:

(1) the context of the health visitor's work in her general duties.

(2) the context in which the health visitor undertakes her school nursing activities.

(3) the functions that the health visitor undertakes as a school nurse.

(4) the time that the health visitor gives to her school nursing and general activities.

Sample: A one in three sample was drawn of health visitors in the county (yielded 60 health visitors); plus wastage allowance of 17 health visitors; (total 72); stratified by health divisions (12 health visitors from each of six divisions). The total number of health visitors involved was 61. A sub-sample of 20 health visitors was interviewed.

Method: Following a pilot study, a letter was sent by the Director of Nursing Services to all health visitors asking them to make notes on their activities as they would be asked about these during the next month. The health visitors were briefed in two sessions and were asked to complete a questionnaire retrospectively for the previous week. Data were also obtained from annual reports and monthly returns. A randomly selected sub-sample of 20 health visitors was interviewed.

Main Findings:

Distribution of time: see Table 2. 10 per cent of the health visitors' time was spent on school nursing duties.

The health visitor on average served four schools and 1,136 pupils.

No medical records were kept at schools, so access to information was limited.

Facilities in schools varied greatly; in 15 per cent of schools the health visitor had exclusive use of a medical room.

The health visitors' work in schools included selection of children for medical inspections (one in six health visitors), follow-up of children needing further observation, recounselling (one in three health visitors).

Researcher's Conclusions: "This study has shown that the health visitor responds with flexibility to the needs of each school and of its pupils and their families".

STUDY NO. 32

Name of Researcher: Walworth-Bell, J. P.

Type of Project: Dissertation submitted for M.Sc (Social Medicine). University of London.

Publication:

(a) "Patchwork: a study of three aspects of the health visitor's work, hypothesising effects on them from how the work is organised, namely either geographically or by attachment to primary care".
M.Sc. dissertation (Social Medicine); University of London 1978. Unpublished.

(b) "Patchwork: a comparative study of the organisation of the work of health visitors". *Health Visitor* 1979, **52**, 8, 307–310.

Date of Study: 1978 (January–March)

Location: London (Greenwich and Bexley Health Districts).

Aims/Purpose of Study:

(1) To compare the visiting workload of "patch" and "attached" health visitors.

(2) To assess the opinions of health visitors of their method of working.

(3) To assess the views of clients on their method of working.

Sample: Two health districts within one AHA were selected for the study; in one (Greenwich) nearly all the health visitors worked on a geographical basis, in the other (Bexley) all the health visitors were attached to general practices.

Method: The sample consisted of all health visitors in both districts (92 health visitors). Response rate: 80 per cent. Data were obtained from 70 health visitors who recorded their work for four weeks.

Method: Information was obtained on all visits over a period of four weeks. Health visitors completed a one-page visiting sheet for every visit made, including the reasons for it, referrals from it, the age of the primary patient and the initiator.

(N.B. a separate part of the study, not included in this review, involved interviews with a sample of parents of nine month old first-born children.)

Main Findings

A "common core" of health visiting practice.

A common concentration of young children.

"Patch" health visitors spent more time on visiting.

Fewer referrals among "patch" health visitors.

Little follow-up or referrals of families known not to have a G.P.

Attached health visitors had more spontaneous consultations on clinic/surgery premises.

Parents' health knowledge was scanty.

Researcher's Conclusions: Both methods of organising a health visitor's work have advantages; some flexibility permitting both "patch" and "attached" organisation simultaneously would be ideal.

Name of Researcher: Watson, P. J.

Type of Project: Ph.D thesis. University of Aberdeen.

Publication:

(a) "A Time Study of Health Visitors' Work". Unpublished Report. Scottish Home and Health Department. (MSRC(77)1/9/1). 1976.

(b) "Studying Work". *Nursing Times* (Occasional Papers). 1979. 75, 20, 81–84.

Date of Study: 1975.

Location: Aberdeen.

Aims/Purpose of Study: Previous studies of health visiting have used self-recorded work records, questionnaires and interviews. "The present study was undertaken in an attempt to increase our knowledge about health visiting using very different techniques—observation and time study".

Sample: Volunteer health visitors. 21 health visitors were observed, each for four consecutive days (564 visits). Not a random sample but it included both male and female health visitors working in a variety of situations and representing a wide range of ages and interests.

Method: A pilot study, using a tape recorder, was used to develop activity and topic classifications.

Prior to the main study, the aims and methods were described at a meeting of all the health visitors in the area and the sample was selected from those who agreed to take part.

The researcher accompanied the health visitor and observed and recorded all activities using the method of cumulative time study developed by Richardson i.e. using a stop watch, the time is recorded at each change of activity, the duration of the activity is subsequently calculated.

Main Findings:

Distribution of time: see Table 2. The range of time spent on home visiting varied from 12 per cent to 46 per cent of total time.

The average duration of a home visit was 17 minutes, compared with 12 minutes per clinic consultation.

Activites: In 52 per cent of visits "listening" was the main activity.

in 22 per cent of visits "questioning" was the main activity.

in 13 per cent of visits "social chat" was the main activity.

in 6 per cent of visits "giving information" was the main activity.

Topics relating to child care were the main source of discussion in 43 per cent of visits.

Researcher's Conclusions:

"Although one can offer little in the way of substantive proof, my impression has been that the material and results obtained portray health visiting in Aberdeen much as it actually is."

"The amount of time spent on those topic groups predominantly related to social care shows that in many instances health visitors *do* function as general purpose social workers despite the protestations of the Seebohm Report."

Name of Researcher: White, W.

Type of Project: Management survey.

Publication: "Survey and Analysis of the Work of the Health Visitor Attached to General Practices in Cardiff." Unpublished Report. City of Cardiff 1972.

Date of Study: November 1971.

Location: Cardiff.

Aims/Purpose of Study:

(1) Analysis of the health visitor workload parameter (mean duration of home visits).

(2) Analysis of workload differential from practice to practice.

(3) To draw up a basic standard of work for general practice health visiting.

(4) To estimate the staffing requirement to maintain the basic standard of health visiting.

Sample: All health visitors working in Cardiff on 1 and 2 November 1971 (number not given); specialist health visitors were included.

Method: Participants recorded the time they spent on each activity on two designated working days (details of the recording method not given). Each health visitor, helped by the nursing officer, gave details of all the cases on her practice list. The health visitor also completed a questionnaire giving details of their views on the minimum number of visits required by the various categories of persons in their practices. The recommended number of visits and the recorded mean duration of a visit were combined with demographic information in a formula to calculate the number of health visitors required to meet the set minimum standard.

Main Findings: (relating to work records only).

Distribution of time: see Table 2.

Average duration of a visit was 13 minutes.

Researcher's Conclusions:

(1) The analysis of the individual workloads illustrates the variety of the health visitor's work.

(2) The calculated number of health visitors required is slightly below the D.H.S.S. recommendation of one health visitor to 3,000 population.

(3) If the required number of health visitors cannot be provided, the standard will inevitably fall unless other ways are found to meet these needs.

STUDY NO. 35

Name of Researchers: Wilkes, J. S. and Nimmo, A. W.

Type of Project: Management survey undertaken by the Operational Research Group, North Eastern Health Services Research and Intelligence Unit, Grampian Health Board.

Publication:

(a) "An Analysis of Work Patterns in Community Nursing".
Nursing Times (Occasional Papers), 1976, 72, 29 January, 13–16, and 1976, 72, 5 February, 17–20.

(b) "Working Patterns in Community Nursing: An Analysis".
Report No. 20. Operational Research Group, North Eastern Health Services Research and Intelligence Unit, Grampian Health Board 1974.

Date of Study: 1972–1975.

Location: Scotland (Inverurie, Peterculter and Ellon).

Aims/Purpose of Study: "Since little is known quantitatively about the work of district nurses or health visitors it is difficult to predict what staff level would be required. . . . As a first approach to this problem of predicting staff levels a clearer picture of working habits was required. . . . It is intended to derive from this study a general formula for staff levels which can be applied in any area according to its geography, population structure and other local characteristics".

Sample: Locations were selected on the basis that a Health Centre had newly opened there, or one was planned to serve that area in the near future. The sample included all health visitors and district nurses (health visitors only included in this review) working in the area concerned.

Peterculter: 3·5 health visitors: two surveys of one week each.

Ellon: two health visitors: two weeks.

Inverurie: two health visitors: two weeks.

Method: Health visitors recorded all their activities during the survey period, using a diary form. "The nurse took the form on her rounds and filled it in as activities took place. All that was required was a tick in the appropriate box for the activity being undertaken and a note of the time of starting it; some room was left for comment if the nurse felt this was necessary".

Main Findings:

The workload of the health visitors varied considerably from day to day; they appear to regulate their work on a weekly rather than a daily basis.

The percentages of visiting time, clinic time and travelling time were similar in the two urban centres, but in the rural centre, more time was spent on visiting and on travel.

There was great individual variation in the duration of visits recorded by different health visitors.

Duration of visits did not depend on the daily workload (in contrast to those of district nurses).

Researchers' Conclusions: Not given.

STUDY NO. 36

Name of Researcher: Wiseman, J.

Type of Project: M.Sc. thesis: University of Lancaster. D.H.S.S. research fellowship.

Publication:

(a) "Health Visiting: the allocation problem". M.Sc. thesis, University of Lancaster 1979. Unpublished.

(b) "Activities and Priorities of Health Visitors". *Nursing Times* (Occasional Papers), 1979, 75, 24, 97–100, and 1979, 75, 25, 101–104.

Date of Study: 1977–78.

Location: Blackpool.

Aims/Purpose of Study: To devise a management tool to aid nurse managers with the allocation of health visiting responsibilities.

To develop a model which will provide target visiting rates for each health visitor such that sector targets will be achieved and the pattern of visiting for each individual health visitor is in line with her interests and priorities.

Sample: All the health visitors in one sector of the health district (25 health visitors). 100 per cent response rate.

Activities were recorded for 40 consecutive working days (eight weeks).

Method: Data for the development of the model were collected in three ways:
(a) Definition of visiting rate requirements for the various care groups in the sector by the use of an allocation plan. The care-group populations within the sector were estimated from various sources such as census data. Nurse managers were asked, by means of interviews, to determine an "ideal" and "minimum" level of health visiting contact with each care-group.
(b) Analysis of the current activities of the health visitors. Data were obtained by means of an "activity questionnaire", which repondents completed for each client contact during a period of 40 consecutive working days.
(c) Discovering the interests and priorities of the health visitors in the sector, by means of an interview.

Main Findings: (Activity survey only).

54 per cent of contacts recorded were with children under five years; 20 per cent were with persons aged over 65 years.

Health visitors initiated 71 per cent of the contacts recorded, 11 per cent of contacts were initiated by the clients or their families, 6 per cent by general practitioners.

Although 24 of the 25 respondents were attached to general practices, only six received regular referrals from G.P.s; these were all based at the same premises as the G.P.s.

The "primary function" most frequently recorded by respondents was "monitoring of client's condition" (55 per cent of all contacts); the most frequently recorded "secondary function" was health education.

Researcher's Conclusions:

50 per cent of health visiting effort is directed towards five per cent of the population (i.e. children under five years). Managers must ask whether this should be maintained or whether health visitors should be encouraged to allocate their time to other of the care group population.

Activity data of the health visitors' contacts and functions to the care groups will help the managers to monitor both the variation from the managerial target objectives as well as the variation from the health visitors' subjective judgements of health visiting priorities.

By taking various aspects of the research data into account the nurse managers will be able to allocate care group target objectives to the health visitors which both conform to the community's need and the health visitors' interests and priority judgements.

STUDY NO. 37*

Name of Researcher: Young, W. C.
Type of Project: Work study project undertaken by employing authority (M.O.H.)
Publication: "A Work Study of Nursing Staff in a Health Department".
Health Bulletin, 1971, 29, 3, 154–161.
Date of Study: November 1969–1970 (March).
Location: Scotland (Burgh of Motherwell and Wishaw).
Aims/Purpose of Study: To examine the work of 44 nurses employed in the Burgh, six months after the attachment of nurses to general practice.
Sample: All nurses employed by the Burgh at the time of the study (20 health visitors). Work was recorded for one week.

Method: Each nurse was randomly allocated a week during which she completed a daily work study form. At the start of each day the starting time of the first activity was entered, followed by a code number for the activity, the place, whether or not the client was at home, and whether or not she thought the activity could have been carried out by a nurse of lesser qualifications. She then proceeded to the next activity, so that the starting times formed a continuum of time throughout the allocation week. The time taken for each activity was subsequently calculated. The mean visit times were converted to "performance targets".

Main Findings:

The health visitors spent 53 per cent of their time in direct contact with clients; they spent 33 per cent on "paediatric care", 8 per cent on "geriatric care", 6 per cent on "obstetric care", 19 per cent on travel, 28 per cent on records and consultation with colleagues, and 6 per cent on other activities.

They spent 42 per cent of their time in the client's home, 35 per cent in the health department, 12 per cent at G.P. surgeries and clinics, 10 per cent at the town council offices and 1 per cent at other places.

The health visitors considered that 2 per cent of their time was spent on activities which could have been entirely carried out by a lesser qualified nurse and 12 per cent partially so.

In 25 per cent of the home visits the client was not at home.

Researcher's Conclusions:

The time spent on "no reply" visits and travel is unacceptably high; the time spent on "geriatric care" is unacceptably low.

The introduction of an acceptable form of self-monitoring can be expected to improve a service and a nursing service is no exception to this.

The mean times for visits and clinic attendances, used as performance targets, might be introduced as a method of monitoring staff performance.

The performance ratios could engender a spirit of competition among the members of a nursing group but there is no harm in this. As far as the administrative staff is concerned, the ratios would provide a measure of overall nursing performance and performance trends, and might indicate whether work was being fairly shared among members of the field staff.

126

References

ARNSTEIN, M. G. (1956). Time Studies of Nursing Activities. In: International Council of Nurses (1956). International Conference on the Planning of Nursing Studies. London, Florence Nightingale International Foundation.

BAILEY, D. AND RAWLINSON, K. (1969). Dictaphones in Health Visiting. Nursing Times 65, 42.

COMMITTEE FOR THE STUDY OF NURSING EDUCATION (1923). Nursing and Nursing Education in the United States: Report of the Committee for the Study of Nursing Education and Report of a Survey by Josephine Goldmark. New York, MacMillan.

COUNCIL FOR THE EDUCATION AND TRAINING OF HEALTH VISITORS (1973). The Health Visitor: Functions and Implications for Training. London, C.E.T.H.V.

FRENCH, R. M. (1968). The Dynamics of Health Care. New York, McGraw-Hill Book Co.

HAWTHORN, P. J. (1971). The Nurse Working with the General Practitioner: an Evaluation of Research and a Review of the Literature. London, D.H.S.S.

HICKS, D. (1976). Primary Medical Care. London, H.M.S.O.

HOBBS, P. (1973). Aptitude or Environment. London, Royal College of Nursing.

HYMAN, H. (1955). Survey Design and Analysis. Glencoe, The Free Press.

JOHNSON, C. et al (1978). Survey into "No Access" Visits by Health Visitors. Health Visitor, 51, 10, 404–405.

JOHNSON, W. L. AND HARDIN, C. (1962). Content and Dynamics of Home Visits and Public Health Nurses. Part I. New York, American Nurses Foundation Inc.

KRAUSZ, E. AND MILLER, S. H. (1974). Social Research Design. London, Longman.

LUKER, K. (1978). Goal Attainment: a Possible Model for Assessing the Role of the Health Visitor. Nursing Times, 74, 30, 1251–1257.

MACGUIRE, J. (1969). Threshold to Nursing. Occasional Papers on Social Administration No. 30. London, G. Bell and Sons Ltd.

MOSER, C. A. AND KALTON, G. (1971). Survey Methods in Social Investigation. (2nd Edition). London, Heinemann Educational Books Ltd.

OPPENHEIM, A. N. (1966). Questionnaire Design and Attitude Measurement. London, Heinemann Educational Books Ltd.

REEDY, B. L. (1976). The Health Team. Medical Care Research Unit. University of Newcastle.

SCHLOTFELDT, R. M. (1975). The Need for a Conceptual Framework. In: Verhonick, P. J. (1975). Nursing Research I. Boston, Little Brown and Co.

STACEY, M. (1969). Methods of Social Research. Oxford, Pergamon Press.

TREECE, E. W. AND TREECE, J. W. (1973). Elements of Research in Nursing. Saint Louis, C. V. Mosby Co.